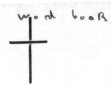

word book

PARISH OF DRUMRAGH
DIOCESE OF DERRY

This book was awarded to

Pamela Ellis

in Class....9......for

ATTENDANCE
and
PROFICIENCY

in Sunday School for the year

ending June, 19..84.

Mr. W. J. E. Dukelow   D. C. Orr
Superintendent   Rector

Dear
Dawn

Dear
Dad

Dear Dawn

Dear Dad

John and Dawn Dobbert

Fleming H. Revell Company
Old Tappan, New Jersey

Library of Congress Cataloging in Publication Data

Dobbert, John.
    Dear Dawn, Dear Dad.

    1. Young women—Conduct of life. I. Dobbert, Dawn, joint author. II. Title.
BJ1681.D59   248.8'33   80-39
ISBN 0-8007-1108-4

TO
Dawn, Denise, and Danelle,
I dedicate the beliefs
expressed in this book
and my continued love and support

Contents

Contents

8   *Contents*

8

Introduction

We sat around the dining-room table, coloring Easter eggs. It was Good Friday, and we were thoroughly enjoying another family tradition. Maybe family traditions are important to kids, but no one needs them or enjoys them more than I do. Playing Santa, trick-or-treating, or coloring eggs, provides me with an opportunity to retreat from the pressures of everyday life and reflect upon God's goodness, shining brightly through the eyes of my daughters. Somehow, today that reflection carried greater significance than ever before.

Dawn, seventeen, although thoroughly engrossed in embossing a Mickey Mouse decal on an egg for her little sister, gave me that perceptive grown-up look, as much as to say, "Isn't it fun appeasing these younger children?"

Denise, fourteen, clumsily dropped another egg into the green dye, only to issue a sigh of relief when she saw the dye land on the spread newspaper, rather than Mom's walnut table. She had recently lost twenty pounds and wondered aloud whether Easter bunnies frequented the health-food store.

Danelle, eleven, was in seventh heaven. As she dunked one egg with her right hand, she reached for another with her left, all the while talking nonstop. Her conversation was diverse, ranging from the question "Does the Easter bunny come at night?" to statements like, "I know Jesus rising from the grave is the most important thing about Easter."

During those delightful two hours, I caught each of their eyes for an instant, and Dad and each daughter experienced a private interlude that caused tears to well up in my eyes. I saw and felt deeply so many things that evening: I saw anxiety and felt responsibility to comfort; I saw excitement and felt responsibility to temper it with reality; I saw creativeness and felt a responsibility to encourage its development; I saw needs and felt the responsibility to provide; I saw faith and felt the responsibility to redirect it toward Christ; I saw fear and felt responsibility to console. Most of all, I saw love and felt the responsibility to accept and return it.

Three daughters, three precious lives—each one was at a different and exciting stage, but within a short time all would be adults. Awed by the sense of tremendous responsibility, I wondered whether the task to guide could be adequately performed by anyone. Could I, in proper perspective and understandable terms, convey to my girls the opportunities, delights, dangers, anxieties, emotions, pressures, new experiences, relationships, responsibilities and all the other variables of the teenage years? Maybe not, but after that evening, I knew I must try. The task couldn't be left to chance.

One night, while thanking God for all my blessings, a somber thought crossed my mind: *What if I should die tonight? I have so many things I haven't said to my daughters.* I don't want them to miss the things that only I, as their dad, may feel. Surely Dottie could raise them well; she has so many talents. Other children make it without a dad. But Dawn, Denise and Danelle, I want to share my thoughts on how to experience true meaning in life.

Although these letters are addressed to Dawn, and she has responded to each, my words are really directed to all three of my daughters, whom I deeply love.

Dear Dawn

Dear Dad

"Hey, Dawn, You're Normal"

Dear Dawn:

During adolescence, the period between childhood and adulthood, new awakenings occur in your mind and new sensations occur in your body. Feelings you've never experienced jolt you frequently, some becoming so intense you can hardly stand them.

Emotions and interests change often and seem to have a three-octave range. Ten minutes ago you were excited and elated but now are depressed and bored, yet nothing observable has happened in the interim. A week ago you were sure you'd train to be a veterinarian, but today you can't even stand the sight of your dog. Today the neighbor's son is just an obstruction in the neighborhood game; a few months from now you'll plot to cross his path.

You speak about being an individual and don't respect those adults who appear so plastic and alike; yet you can't wear that dress when all the others are wearing slacks, can't wear your hair short when the majority of your class has long hair, can't have Dad drive you to the game when friends are walking, because being different at this age hurts.

You want attention and often act to get it, but when it's focused on you, you don't know how to handle it. You just know everyone's looking at you if your nose is a little different, pants are a quarter inch short, or there's a space between your teeth.

Meeting new people affords many problems, but the biggest faced is, "Where do I look?" Your eyes may be fixed over his head, to his left, to her right, but, at all costs, you must avoid face-to-face contact.

Often time seems to fly, and yet when you're waiting for that special event (your learner's permit, your first date, your sixteenth birthday, or the vacation with friends), time seems to stand still for eons.

You can't believe the unreasonable demands made upon your time by your mom, dad, teachers, church leaders, and other adults, yet any friend can be granted a five-hour audience at a moment's notice.

Favorite friends change frequently. On Sunday it's Sue, but by Wednesday she's out of the top forty because of something she did on Tuesday. Rock music blares from your room throughout the entire house, yet someone quietly doing something you've decided not to accept drives you to distraction. Depending on your mood, you can cry at Charlie Brown, yet sit unaffected while viewing a tearjerker. At times you feel special, but *special* turns to *nothing special* before the instant replay shows.

Mom and Dad have been heard to utter: "When are you ever going to grow up?" "When I was your age I. . . ." "You sure have it better than I had it." "Act like a grown-up." Please understand that these statements are spoken in frustration, but love. You see, we parents don't know if we're equal to the task either; but God has given you to us, and we're trying to do the job the best way we know how.

Some kids worry that they'll inherit too many attributes of their mom or dad. As parents, some of our inadequate attempts are motivated by this same fear. If we had our way, we'd like you to sort out and adopt our admirable qualities, discard some other qualities, and integrate the good with your specialness.

You're taller than some, heavier than some, more mature than some, less mature than others, achieve more than some; you're not as good an athlete as others, more emotional than some, stronger than others, a favorite of your French teacher, a burden to your geometry teacher, a consumer of junk foods, and many other things. *But* above all, as you go through your teen years, be comforted by the fact that you're *normal*. Other teens, if honest, would admit that they're experiencing the same thoughts and feelings. Even though you're normal, you are still unique and special. God has made only one of you, and there are contributions to life that only *you* can make.

> *Lovingly,*
> DAD

P.S. Can you read this passage from God's Word without feeling special?

> You made all the delicate, inner parts of my body, and knit them together in my mother's womb. Thank you for making me so wonderfully complex! It is amazing to think about. Your workmanship is marvelous—and how well I know it. You were there while I was being formed in utter seclusion! You saw me before I was born and scheduled each day of my life before I began to breathe. Every day was recorded in your Book! How precious it is, Lord, to realize you are thinking about me constantly! I can't even count how many times a day your thoughts turn towards me. And when I waken in the morning, you are still thinking of me!
>
> Psalms 139:13–18

Dear Daddy:

You have hit upon so many of my feelings.

Adolescence has been the most confusing period of my life. I'm frustrated when I'm unable to diagnose the causes of my moodiness and frequent emotional changes. Just when I feel I'm beginning to understand myself and my reason for doing things, I take a course of action that makes little or no sense.

At times, for no apparent reason, I become very emotional. I've almost given up on stability, for my moods and interests seem to change as often as the weather. The interests I had six months ago have changed, and gone full circle.

I experience many fears that even *I* know are irrational but, nevertheless, exist. Right now it is extremely important for me to be accepted by those with whom I come into contact. I hate to be different, for fear my differences will be the focus of people's attention, yet I hope I'm not just a carbon copy of every other teenager. I am overly conscious of my physical appearance and often feel that each person who passes notices every imperfection I have.

Daddy, thanks for assuring me that others have these feelings and that I am normal and made unique by God's own hand.

Please don't worry about my inheriting your less-than-admirable qualities. You, too, must accept the fact that God created you just as you are. Trust Him to guide my selection of the many special qualities you possess.

Love,
DAWN

Be Yourself—Be Strong

Dear Dawn:

You'll feel pressure to be one of the group, yet I ask you to be yourself. When this situation occurs, you may feel a conflict raging within; but strength comes from weighing the consequences and doing what you feel is correct, even at the expense of being set aside by the group.

Wearing the same kind of clothes as your peers, going to the same recreational activities as your friends, and being consistent with others are all important to you during these teen years. You have my blessing if these things make you feel good and aren't against our family's principles. I don't consider these desires unreasonable or of earth-shattering importance. But, Dawn, be yourself, and do what you know is right, even when doing wrong is easier and more popular.

When friends are taking part in an activity you know is wrong, I expect you to leave. You needn't announce your departure in some pious manner, such as saying, "I must leave because you're doing wrong." They'll know why you left and respect you for it. You'll not even have to defend your position. Weakness follows, even when in doubt. Strength leads.

It's always easy to follow the crowd, but growth comes when you stand strong, guided by your convictions (your feelings of what is right or wrong for you, personally). Pilate knew Jesus was the Saviour, but gave in to the pressure of an angry crowd and allowed Jesus to be crucified. This decision had an effect on all of history.

Your ability to say "No," even though the crowd says, "Go ahead," will affect your whole life.

As I work with kids every day, I recognize the most feeble excuse to be, "Well, all the other kids were doing it." Some time ago, I watched six boys handcuffed and taken to juvenile hall. One had decided to rob a house, yet five tagged along, just to be accepted. They didn't want to say "No."

As you mature, attempt to avoid group decisions in which your input is not considered; but if you're a part of the group, always speak your piece if you disagree with the decision you feel is about to be made. Trying to live your life in a manner which would please others is a dead-end street, leading to worry and frustration.

Learn to say "No." Although *no* sounds negative, it can be the most positive word in your development into the person God and I want you to be.

No, not *maybe*, should be clearly stated when you are asked to take part in, or even be around, any activity which you know is wrong for you. Your *no* can also be stated without a word, as you leave the activity. Don't worry about losing friends by saying, "No." You'll find that many others will meet you on that new plateau. "Cream always rises to the top."

And you know what? The feeling you'll get by making the right decision will fill your heart to overflowing. Joy comes through knowing you've made the decision which is best for you.

When you doubt your ability to stand up and make the right decision, remember that God has promised to give you the necessary strength.

Thanks, Dawn, for being yourself and carefully considering

the choices you make. Making correct choices at this age will lay a foundation for correct choices in the future.

Love,

DAD

Dear Daddy:

At some time or another I'm sure every teenager has said, "Everybody has one," or, "Everyone else is doing it." When we say this, most parents respond with the question, "Everybody?" Thanks for explaining that weakness follows and strength leads. I do want to be strong.

Sometimes I feel pressure from you and Mom to go places or participate in activities that I know aren't right; yet, because you don't know what happens at those gatherings, you still insist. Please trust my judgment when I say I'd rather not go. I'm not confronted with this problem frequently, because of my choice of friends.

I do get upset, though, when you restrict me from some activities based on the reasoning, "You've done enough for one day." This statement really puts a limit on the enjoyment I can experience, and at times I feel it's unjust. It especially bothers me when I've spent much time at home and really pitched in with the work to be done. Sometimes I think you restrict me because you think that the amount of freedom I have will reflect on you, or you must demonstrate your authority over me.

Because God *has* placed me under your authority, I will abide by your decisions. Please understand, though: I'll soon be on my own and will be responsible for my own decisions. I believe you could relax your controls on me and slowly grant me more independence, so I'm prepared to make those decisions and not confronted with that responsibility all at once. If I didn't know you trusted me, I'd believe your tight control meant you didn't.

Love,

DAWN

Slow Down and Enjoy Yourself

Dear Dawn:

Working with teenagers the last sixteen years, I have noticed one consistent strain. All seem to possess a strong desire to grow up quickly and partake in the privileges of adulthood.

Unfortunately, most kids forget that with adult privileges come heavy responsibilities, responsibilities which you will bear most of your life, from the moment you accept them.

I've seen marriages at sixteen. At first the friends of the couple think it's glamorous and view the bride and groom with envy. Two years later, when that young lady should still be enjoying her freedom and bursting with excitement as she views her many career opportunities, she's saddled down with the responsibility of raising two children and maintaining an apartment which can barely be afforded.

If I could get this one point across I'd be happy. Even though you have a strong desire to mature and experience everything adult, slow down and be a kid for a while longer.

After the short-lived glamour of partaking in the adult world, the newness of the experiences will wear off, and you will awaken to find the many responsibilities you've accepted too early are heavily taxing and tend to rob you of your youthful joy and exuberance.

Remember how excited you were to run all my errands when you first received your driver's license? It doesn't take

long for the thrill to subside and become a routine happening.
Remember that.

I want you to accept responsibility and, with God's help,
will give you more and more as you continue to mature, but
don't be too anxious to bite off a bundle.

What appear to be glamorous, newly granted freedoms, at
first, often turn to resentment as you view your friends, still
free to make choices, while you are already committed for life.

Early commitments greatly reduce your future choices.
You'd like to return to school, but you moved out and rented
your own apartment. You know rent payments must be met,
so the desire to further your education must be set aside and
will most likely never become a reality. Accept your responsibilities in small doses and carefully examine all decisions
mandating life commitments.

In America, it often seems as though we parents are dying to
shove you out of the house as early as possible, to make you
an adult. I want you to know you're welcome to take advantage of the security and love our home offers, until you've
carefully weighed the important decisions and are ready to act.

I will expect you to continue assuming your fair share of responsibilities at home, however, since accepting responsibility
on this scale prepares you for the long-term responsibilities
which are just around the corner.

When any doubt surrounds those decisions, be my little girl
a little longer and bask in my love until you're assured the decision is a good one.

Slow down and enjoy yourself.

Love,
DAD

Dear Daddy:

How soon you forget! I bet you and your generation were just as anxious as we are to try everything adult.

My feelings about this subject almost seem to fluctuate daily. Sometimes I can't wait to move out (usually after a hassle) but minutes later, just the thought of leaving frightens me. I'm glad that in a few years I'll have the opportunity to experiment with independence at college. Those four years should provide me with the chance to see if I can really handle the problems that confront me, before I cut the ties.

I often feel as though I'm obligated to prove myself worthy of two successful parents by becoming more responsible and independent. Although it is not obvious to you, your accomplishments frequently provoke feelings of inadequacy within me. These effects aren't always negative though, for they provide me with an additional desire to succeed.

I don't believe you'll have to worry about my growing up and leaving too quickly. The security your home offers will always be welcome.

Your little girl,
DAWN

My Parents Said, "No"

Dear Dawn:

Boy, it's difficult to be a parent! The easiest thing in the world is to say, "Yes, do what you want to do and leave Dad and Mom out of it." And yet I could never live with that, because I have a responsibility to bring you up well.

At times we'll differ about whether or not you should take part in an activity. After we discuss it, I may change my mind if you've convinced me that you're capable of handling the situation which I doubted you could handle. As you demonstrate your ability to accept more responsibility wisely, I will grant you additional responsibilities. But, in the meantime, during your teenage years, you can expect many *nos*.

No is a hard word for me to say. Our culture has taught us that if we love someone we say, "Yes," and *no* is negative, so it must be associated with lack of love; but this is not the case. I say, "No," to you often, because I love you.

If I believe you should not go with the group to a certain function, I will say, "No." Part of my reason for saying, "No," might be that I don't think you're ready to handle the pressures I believe will exist at that particular party or gathering. I may have guessed wrong, and you may well have been able to handle the situation, but maybe you haven't had an opportunity to demonstrate that to me. We may have missed each other when you were showing how responsible you were in that particular respect.

I may say, "No," when you're asked to go on a short trip, and I know Fred is driving. I may say, "No," because I've seen Fred drive and because he has exhibited carelessness and recklessness behind the wheel of his car. You mean too much to me to let that lack of judgment snuff out your life.

Please never misconstrue the fact that I'm saying, "No," to mean, "I don't trust you." The noes are part of my responsibility, and slowly those noes will turn to yeses as you mature, for I realize that it is necessary to let go of the reins so you can assume more independence. I hope we can coordinate this process effectively, for when you're ready to leave home I want you fully to be able to make effective and sound decisions.

Please let me know, honey, when you see I am hanging on to the reins too tightly and too long. Let's talk about this. After our discussion, I may believe you are right and make some adjustments, for I am human and err often; but, after discussing it, I may very well say, "No, I've made the right decision, and I believe it has to stay this way for now."

Being able to accept what I say requires some trust on your part. You may be "bent out of shape," or you may be angry because the rest of your friends are going while I withhold permission. Even when I consent to your going with the rest of the gang, however, I will always demand to know where you're going, who you are going with, and what time you are going to be in, and if the answers to these questions do not meet with my approval, I will have to say, "No."

I love you, and one day, when you love someone as much as I love you, only then will you realize the importance of the word NO.

Love,
DADDY

Daddy,

I understand that saying, "No," is sometimes an act of love. At times, however, I feel you and other parents use *no* when you're afraid. The fear of exposing their daughters to something that is possibly harmful, the fear of appearing too lenient to other parents, and most of all, the fear that their daughters are growing up, prompts many *noes*.

It disappoints me when I feel you don't trust my judgment in these areas. It occasionally is embarrassing when my friends are allowed to participate in an activity and I'm not. It makes me feel less mature and less trusted than my peers. I know my limitations and capabilities and will not enter into anything that may be self-destructive.

I know you love me, but please don't let your fears and overconcern for me force you to say, "No," too often, to many activities that add so much to my high-school years and make me feel more adult.

When you say, "No," I'll obey you because you are my dad; God expects me to; and I love you. But please take time to examine my request before you say, "No." To know you thoughtfully considered my request before answering *yes* or *no* makes me feel important and proud to be your daughter.

Love,
DAWN

Doing Your Own Thing

Dear Dawn:

"Doing your own thing" has become a popular and overused cliché in our society. If you listen carefully, you'll hear: "As long as it doesn't hurt anyone else, who cares what I do?" "I should be capable of calling my own shots." "Don't bug me."

I've heard these statements, as I'm sure you have. In fact, I've said them a few times and actually felt like telling everyone around, even my loved ones, to bug off and let me do my own thing.

Yet I've discovered an alarming truth. When I do anything, whether it's dictated by my superiors or decided by me, it always has an effect on others.

The girl who says, "I want to do my own thing regarding sex," and then gets pregnant, involves many: The life of her baby, her parents, the father, those who may have to house her and pick up the welfare tab, all are involved through her decision to "do her own thing."

Remember, as you make decisions, that all your actions will, to some extent, affect the lives of others. I don't tell you this to put undue pressure upon you, for pressure abounds in our society. I only remind you of this fact, so you may become accustomed to thinking of others. One who truly thinks only of himself is egocentric and often shunned by others, while one who considers those around him is cherished as a friend.

As Christians we must do God's thing, not ours. Only when we're sensitive to His Holy Spirit and seek His wisdom and guidance in our decisions are we assured of their being good ones.

I'm proud of most of the decisions you've made and thankful that the majority have positively affected others. As you grow older and your life becomes entwined with other important persons, decisions will become more complex, and each seems to involve greater significance. Even though God has blessed you with common sense, at times you'll doubt your capability to sort out the facts and make the best decision. This happens to your mom and dad as well.

I'd encourage you to refrain from making decisions at night, when the darkness closing in around you seems to be accompanied by all sorts of negative feelings and doubts. It's difficult for most people to make effective decisions at night, since weariness subjects one to an inordinate number of negative emotions. V. Raymon Edman, whom I learned to love while in college, used to say, "Do not doubt in the dark what God has made plain in the light." Refrain from making that decision until the sunlight illuminates the earth, bringing confidence to your spirit and soul and reinforcing your knowledge that He is in control of this new day.

As His children, we have a distinct advantage when we are experiencing times of indecision. He has promised, "If you want to know what God wants you to do, ask him, and he will gladly tell you, for he is always ready to give a bountiful supply of wisdom to all who ask him; he will not resent it" (James 1:5).

So, Dawn, never forget to depend on Him and pray to Him for directions in your decision. I have found that my decisions are far better when I involve Him than when I try to do it on my own.

The great thing about being His is that He encourages us to come to Him, no matter how insignificant we feel the problem or decision is. Sometimes I have disappointed you by claiming, by my words or actions, that your problems or anxieties were silly or nothing to worry about. I ask your forgiveness for that, since I know they were ever so real to you.

As hard as I try, I will disappoint you and fail to understand you, as will Mom, your husband-to-be, and every other human. Only Jesus Christ will never fail you. Each of our concerns is significant to Him. Trust Him.

Love,
DADDY

Dear Daddy:

These feelings of wanting to "do my own thing" have often plagued me. In fact, when you first asked me to consider writing this book, I felt that way. I was tempted to say, "I have so much to do; sometimes I wish you'd just leave me alone. I feel the pressures of homework, church activities, and all. Why do you mention projects like this to me?" I questioned myself then, but now realize how meaningful the writing has been, and thank you for your perseverance.

I agree with you that every decision we make affects others. The statement "you're only hurting yourself" isn't really valid when you finally realize your life is intertwined with others.

Thank you for the insights about decision making. Things which seem so bleak and hopeless at night always do look better in the morning. But I must not use this as an excuse to become a procrastinator.

It is so neat to think that when all others fail us, Jesus Christ won't! Please continue to remind me of that fact as I face difficult decisions. Recently I was comforted when I read, "Casting all your care upon him; for he careth for you" (1 Peter 5:7 KJV). What a great promise!

Love,
DAWN

Self-Esteem

Dear Dawn:

One of the most common problems which surfaces in people is the feeling of inferiority. These feelings about ourselves often begin in childhood, plague us through our teen years, hinder our effectiveness as adults, and finally accompany us to our grave.

You've probably heard the statement, "You are what you think." Although this statement seems far too simplistic, it contains great truth, for most of us are actually bound by the mental limitations we place on ourselves. If you begin your tennis match with the belief that your opponent's skills are superior to yours, nine times out of ten you will lose, even if, in actuality, you're the better player. If your intelligence is such that you earn all A's, yet your mind tells you that you're unable to comprehend mathematical concepts, you'll have a very difficult time handling your math class.

Even God's Word says, "As a man thinketh in his heart, so he is" (*see* Psalms 23:7). Our minds and beliefs about ourselves are so powerful that our Creator says we will be what our mind tells us we are. Our minds can limit us or encourage us to stretch our capabilities; since they to a large degree, determine what we are, it follows that our potential to become more would increase if we could convince our minds that we were worth more.

Unfortunately, I believe Christians often have poorer self-concepts than non-Christians. It's difficult to be described as a "worm" and a "wretch" and hear that your best is no better than "filthy rags" and come out feeling good about yourself, much less having a healthy self-concept.

Only in recent years has it been recognized that a person who loves himself functions more effectively and experiences a greater degree of fulfillment from life. We feel guilty when we begin to feel okay about ourselves, since that borders on pride, and the Bible cautions us against the dangers of pride.

Dawn, I want you to know that it's healthy to love yourself and that God expects you to do so. If you don't love yourself after reading the truths which follow, you are not getting God's message:

> You have been created by the hand of God in His image.
> You have been created a "little lower than the angels."
> You have been given dominion over the earth.
> Even when we were in sin, God gave His own Son (the ultimate value) to provide a way for you to spend eternity with Him.
> God has assigned angels to guard over you.
> God has prepared a mansion for you.
> God has loved you as much as He loved His Son.

If you were worthless, would God have really focused all this attention on you?

Since you are loved by God, you are also deserving of your own love. You may think that loving yourself is really pride and therefore is wrong. On the contrary, loving yourself is not pride. Pride only enters the picture when your attitude becomes one of superiority.

True self-love is when you value yourself as equal in importance to other members of God's creation.

Dawn, the love of God to us allows us to love ourselves.

Only when we love ourselves do we dare reach out to love others. Only if we love ourselves can we approach our potential, for we see ourselves possessing characteristics and faith worth sharing.

I love you and hope you do, too.

Love,
DADDY

Daddy:

You've probably already noticed that I tend to be my own worst enemy when it comes to self-esteem. I occasionally degrade myself to the point where I feel worthless and miserable. I so convince myself I'm below par that I sometimes feel people who compliment me are "putting me on."

I believe most people experience these doubts about themselves, but I'm not sure to what degree. It seems so important to be one of the best in junior high and high school, yet I look around, and there always seems to be so many who are better. Making comparisons doesn't help me feel good about myself.

While I know how miserable it is to be in the company of a conceited person, it must be just as bad to be around me at those times when I'm down on myself. Most of my worries about inadequacy are completely unfounded, and yet they result in hours of needless anxiety and seem so real at the time.

I'm finally learning that people who don't accept me as I am are probably not the kind of people I'd like to have as friends, anyway.

Daddy, thanks for helping me realize that the ultimate judge of my worth is God, not man. That assures me of getting a "fair shake."

Only recently have I noticed that the attitude we have towards ourselves is clearly reflected in our appearance and conduct. As an ambassador of Christ I must therefore first love myself before I can effectively love others.

How good it feels to know of the concern and love God has for me. I must be pretty special and should really be thankful.

Daddy, thanks for letting me know I'm special to you, too.

DAWN

Love

Dear Dawn:

I love you. I'm so glad we use the word *love* with such ease in our home. I'm told that some people live years at a time without telling someone "I love you." Many of those same people are never on the receiving end of an "I love you," either. How tragic.

What's love all about anyway? When your mom and I decided we wanted to have a child, we were excited by the thought of a new little person sharing our lives. What a thrill I had as Mom met me at the door and proudly announced, "I'm pregnant. You're going to be a father."

From that moment on, I loved you. Even though you were diminutive and deep inside Mom's body, I loved you, for you were part of Mom and part of me, conceived in love. You were formed when your mom and dad were physically expressing their deep love for each other.

A few months later, your heartbeat was confirmed, giving me cause for further rejoicing. Then I felt you move, as over and over you rolled, while periodically kicking my hand, which I had laid on Mom's stomach, longing to feel the same thrills of movement she had experienced so subtly for months. You and I were finally in contact. As the months rolled on, I felt I knew you and longed for your arrival, to express the sense of deep love I was experiencing.

Then it happened. The joy of knowing you had arrived

safely and Mom was fine, overwhelmed me. The scene is as vivid today as it was seventeen years ago. As I stood looking through the nursery window, the nurse lifted you up and brought you closer, so I could have a better look. The tears welled in my eyes and rolled down my cheeks. I was overcome with love. You were finally here—the one we'd waited for so long.

No one asked me to love you, nor did I have to think about the option. You were mine, a gift of God, and with your birthright came unconditional love. Seventeen years have come and gone, and many rewarding and fine experiences have passed, but my love for you has been and will continue to be. Life would be a sham without love. I can't even imagine the hollowness of a loveless life.

Just as my love for you is unconditional, so is God's love for us. We didn't have to do a thing to earn God's love. We were immersed in it from the second we began developing. Even if we never responded to God's love, it would still have been extended to us in full intensity.

Many, down through the ages, have attempted to live a worthy life by striving to keep God's Ten Commandments. Yet God demonstrated the great significance of love when He stated, "The commandments . . . are summed up in this one rule: 'Love your neighbor as yourself' " (Romans 13:9 NIV).

He then gave instructions to love, when He declared:

> Dear friends, let us practice loving each other, for love comes from God and those who are loving and kind show that they are the children of God, and that they are getting to know him better. But if a person isn't loving and kind, it shows that he doesn't know God—for God is love.
>
> 1 John 4:7, 8

I thank God that I have the assurance you all know God. Therefore you have access to His love. Only when you love yourself, however, through realizing how He loves you, can you love your neighbor as yourself. The love of God brings self-respect to you and allows you to reach out, beyond your comfort zone, to those you may not even like.

I've been so pleased when I've observed your love for God, for Mom and me, for your sisters, and others. When recently I saw you reach out to the girl whose mom was dying of cancer, at your own expense, in spite of your busy schedule, I was thrilled. When your sister cuddled the new girl, who was being picked on by the older children on the school playground, I was moved. These are practical, everyday demonstrations of love, which please your heavenly Father and your earthly father.

The love which allows us to love others without expecting anything in return is a love which emanates from God. Because He abides within us, we possess God's love potential.

At times we feel our love benefits only those toward whom it is directed, but that is far from the truth. The greatest recipient in giving love is the giver. Let me demonstrate the fact through the following illustration.

Two bodies of water are fed by the Jordan River. One body, the Sea of Galilee, is teeming with life. The sea is abundant with fish, and the surrounding gentle slopes are fertile with figs, olives, dates, and pomegranates. Many people derive their living from the potential the sea possesses. It was by the Sea of Galilee that Jesus fed the five thousand. The other body of water is the Dead Sea. No fish survive its salinity, and very little activity graces its shoreline. Its stagnancy reaffirms the fact that it has appropriately been named the Dead Sea. What causes the difference? How can the same vibrant river result in two bodies of water displaying opposite characteristics? The answer is simple. The Sea of Galilee has an outlet, and the Dead Sea does not.

We can learn an important lesson from God's creation of these two bodies of water. Two people may both have experienced new birth through Jesus Christ, and therefore both have access to His great love. If one of the two fails to reach out to others with love, he will become as stagnant as the Dead Sea, and few people, if any, will be attracted to him. If the second person reaches out to others with love, vitality and life enter his being, and much fulfilling activity will characterize his life.

Dawn, the Lord is "right on" when He says, "This is my commandment, That ye love one another, that your joy may be full" (*see* John 15:11, 12). Your joy will be dependent upon your willingness to reach out to others in love.

Stay close to God. Read His Word; pray and fellowship with other Christians so that your source of love is flowing freely. Then reach out to others in love and expect joy, blessings, and fulfillment to enter your life.

Love,
DADDY

Dear Daddy:

Thank you for sharing that special time with me. Tears flooded *my* eyes and rolled down *my* cheeks as I read it.

Love is usually used with ease in our home. Lately, however, I have fallen into the habit of using *hate* far too frequently. I apologize for this. Please understand that my "hate feelings" are not directed at you personally, but at the decision you've just made or the restriction you've placed on me. That does not excuse my actions, but, with God's help and an increased understanding of your decisions, I know my attitude and feelings will change.

Your illustration involving the Sea of Galilee and the Dead

Sea was meaningful to me. If I hoard my love, I will become spiritually stagnant. On the other hand, I know I cannot continually put out love, without a source for refilling. This could result in my drying up. A time alone with God daily can prevent this tragedy. Pray that I may consistently take time to read the Bible, meditate, and pray.

Thank you, Daddy, for your continual assurance of your love. You not only express it verbally, but every day your actions substantiate it.

Love,
DAWN

So You Call Them Friends?

Dear Dawn:

At no time do your friends seem more important than during your teenage years. I sure like your friends. If I had picked them out myself, I couldn't have done a better job or been more pleased.

Maybe the best advice I could give you is to select all your future friends in the same manner as you've selected your present ones. Although your friends seem important now, as you pass through your teenage years, they take on even more importance, for many of the friends you have during your teen years will be friends for life.

A friend is a person for whom you feel love and warmth. When you're with them you feel good, and after they've left you feel better than before they came. A friend adds to your life and never pressures you to take part in questionable activities. You can talk to a friend openly without undue concern about hurting her feelings. She can even understand when you have a need to be alone. Friends do not leave when you have a problem or when they cannot use you for their personal gain. Friends come in all shapes, colors, sizes, ages and nationalities. I love some of your older friends. It's really neat to see that beauty exists in a friend of eighty years of age, as much as it does in one of your teenage classmates.

I hope your mom and I are your friends as well as your parents. Do you realize that the two of us are friends who truly enjoy each other? Being friends is an important part of having a successful marriage. One of the neatest things about friends is that each of them makes a contribution to your life. You can't help but be better after being with a true friend.

At times you have acted as if you could have only one close friend at a time. This is not the case, for each friend contributes something different to your life, and you, in your unique way, contribute something different to hers. If you desire one friend exclusively, and she solely seeks your companionship, you limit each other's growth, for exclusivity limits the good things you could gain through your contact with many people.

I'm glad you have so many good friends. It reinforces my feeling that you are fun to be around and that God has given you special talents and warmth which attract people to you.

Although I'm very thankful for your earthly friends, I'm also thankful that you have the greatest Friend of all in Jesus Christ. Last Sunday, as we sang "What a Friend We Have in Jesus," I thought how fortunate I am to know that my three girls and my wife and I can truly say we have a personal Friend in Jesus Christ, One to whom we can go with every need, with every concern, and One who is interested in every detail of our lives.

Never forget that earthly friends will occasionally fail you, and you'll even be disappointed in your mom, dad, and brothers, and sisters, but you'll never be disappointed in Jesus Christ. He is closer than a brother and can provide wisdom, strength, and courage, while nurturing the abilities necessary to handle every situation.

If you had no friends on earth, aside from Jesus, He would be all-sufficient to provide for your every need. Let Him know how much He's appreciated, by spending more time with Him.

Love,
DAD

Dear Daddy:

I agree with you and your statement regarding friends and their importance during the high-school years. The people I have chosen as companions can determine my reputation, social standing, and popularity.

Thank you for stressing the point about exclusiveness. Just last week, I learned how much my life revolves around one person. Linda, my closest friend, was sick with the flu and missed two days of school. During those two days, I was with other friends and noticed that, while I preferred her company to others, we both were being deprived of special qualities other people had to offer. Linda and I have the neatest friendship, but I now realize we can enrich and strengthen it even more by better understanding others. Exclusiveness is not harmful if taken in small doses, but an overdose may be fatal.

Daddy, one of the most helpless feelings is to watch close friends straying from what they know is right. A few days ago I felt like crying as I listened to three of my friends deciding who was going to drive, so the other two could get drunk. First Corinthians 15:33 has shown me that I must break away from them, not as an enemy, but out of concern for myself and what the Lord wants for my life. Perhaps someday they'll realize that happiness isn't achieved through such practices. God has instilled in me a great love for them. Pray that I'll be able to express it and not condemn them for their actions.

Daddy, thanks also for emphasizing the security and friendship Jesus Christ offers. When others fail me, it's nice to be reminded He won't.

Love,
DAWN

Okay, Then, I Quit

Dear Dawn:

One of the biggest problems for teenagers is the fact that when things get tough they just up and say, "I quit." I often hear, "School is a bore; I quit." "I don't like the teacher; I quit." Teenagers often think that as long as things go well and smoothly everything is fine, and they'll continue, but if they hit a snag, each says, "I quit."

Quitting sets a dangerous precedent. If, as a teenager, you quit when things do not go well, you'll quit as a young adult, and you'll quit as a middle-aged adult, and you'll quit as an older adult. Quitting becomes a pattern. I can't overemphasize the importance of working through snags and problems.

Growth as an individual always involves some risk and some discomfort, but each time you successfully work through and conquer a problem that has you on the border of quitting, you're better able to handle future challenges.

The opposite is also true. Every time you quit it becomes easier to quit the next time, and the time after that, until you walk away from the smallest problems. If you could trace the life of a quitter, you'd probably see a person who, during the beginning part of his teenage years, was displeased with a certain class, because it required an oral report; so he went to see the counselor to try to quit that class and was successful. Later he obtained a paper route; but, because that paper route was extended to cover a few more blocks, and it interfered with his free time, he quit that paper route, even though he needed the money. In high school, the work required took too much time, so upon reaching sixteen he quit high school. The pattern was set, and when his boss told him he wasn't working hard enough on his first full-time job, he quit. Soon he got married, but when communication problems arose in the marriage, he didn't attempt to work these out. He quit and left two kids and a wife to fend for themselves. Quitting can be as addicting as drugs. It can also be as detrimental.

I'm glad that you and your sisters are children of God, but many Christians believe that once they belong to God's family, life will be a rose garden, completely problem free. However, Christ did not promise us a rose garden and even indicated that we would have snags; yet He promised that these snags, trials, and temptations are put in our lives for a purpose. They are present to teach us patience and long-suffering and to build character in our lives. Christ also gave us a provision to allow us to conquer this temptation to quit, for we can claim the promise that Paul claimed, "We can do all things through Christ who strengthens us" (*see* Philippians 4:13).

Dawn, remember that, when the going seems rough and you're tempted to quit. Pray about it and discuss it honestly with God. Let Him know your concerns, your difficulties, and that you feel like quitting, but then ask Him to fulfill His promise to provide strength to help you meet and defeat that temptation to quit.

His strength is sufficient for all our needs, including the need to conquer the tendency to quit.

Jesus Christ established a pattern for us to follow. He followed through with every task to its completion and then declared, "It is finished."

Keep on truckin'.

DAD

P.S. I thoroughly enjoyed the note you left on my dresser last week: "Dear Mom & Dad: Finished sewing the pair of slacks tonight. My zipper only took four hours. (At least you can't say I'm a quitter—an idiot maybe, but not a quitter.) Love, Dawn."

Dear Daddy:

So many times I have resented your authority in this area! You have never allowed me to duck an assignment or presentation or quit an activity, even though I was very uncomfortable and was seeking a way out. I've pleaded, cried, and stomped, but you stood firm. At the time I couldn't understand your reasoning, but lately it has become apparent to me. Through each incident I have been strengthened. I have no doubt that in the future I'll occasionally feel the same way, but I'm praying that God will not let me forget my past experiences.

You've omitted what I feel is one of the major reasons for quitting among teenagers: laziness. So many times I've wanted to quit because it's not convenient or something I truly enjoy doing. I have discovered that if I push myself and continue participating in the questionable area, God seems to bless me more and more. I had a real desire to quit the tennis team this year, but stuck with it. As a result I've improved my skills, strengthened my self-control, and made many new friends.

God has promised us an abundant life, and I'm learning to see that these trials are a part of it. I shudder to think what would have happened if God had quit. I'm sure He became very frustrated with the sin of Adam and Eve, but I'm glad He didn't just say, "Forget it." Please pray for me to have more discipline in the future, when I'm not under your authority, to hang in there and not be a quitter.

Love,
DAWN

Sex: Beauty or Tragedy?

Dear Dawn:

As I left my hotel room this morning and walked through the Tenderloin District of San Francisco, I became vividly aware of the abuse and misuse of sex. Every newspaper openly displayed it. Every billboard advertised it, and women and men walked the streets, openly seeking customers with whom to share sexual experiences for money. I was heartsick as I thought of you growing up in a society which has drifted away from the beauty of sex that God intended.

Is there a conflict? On the one hand, our society is obsessed with sex; we smear it on the screen, use it for commercial enticement, and yet expect you, as a teenager, to develop healthy, wholesome, constructive attitudes toward sex. We adults really haven't set a very good example, and I apologize to you for that.

I hope, however, that you have had a good example set here at home. I hope you see and feel love. I realize that the values you develop toward sex most often are a reflection of your teaching in the home. When we first brought you home from the hospital, we tried to immerse you in love. We held you frequently. You enjoyed it to such a degree that pretty soon we had a hard time setting you down without having you scream bloody murder. Soon, you had us trained. From that day to this, we have tried to show you love in many ways.

We realize it feels good to be loved, good to be touched,

good to be caressed, and good to be kissed. All of these things bring pleasure, and God intended for them to bring pleasure. He alone has given us these desires and needs. He wants our desires to be fulfilled in pleasure and has given us a plan for that to happen.

When, after a courtship period, you marry the person you deeply love, you'll experience one of the highest pleasures in life when you give yourself sexually to him. God expects you and your new husband to become one and to share sexual intimacy in full enjoyment.

Between that time and this, you will have to make many decisions: When a boy takes me out, should I let him kiss me? Should I kiss him back? If he tries to pet, should I allow it? If I don't do it, will he drop me and never ask me out again?

Only you can answer these questions. I can give you some guidelines, but I will not be with you in the backseat of the car when your new boyfriend asks you to become intimate. At that point, all I can do is pray that what you have learned at home and at church will be sufficient to allow you to make the right decision.

I've heard sex compared to fire. When a fire is in a fireplace, on a cold, wintry night, and we are huddled in front of it to enjoy its warmth, it is a beautiful thing. On the other hand, when we're helplessly standing in the street watching our house and all its possessions burn to the ground, fire can be a tragic thing.

Sex is much the same. If it is used as God intended it to be used, it can add greatly to the marriage relationship and can provide a beautiful, intimate experience which adds great dimension and depth to the feeling between two people. If, however, it is used loosely, it can add heartbreak, anxiety, concern, negativism, and tragedy to your life. There's something very special about saving yourself for that special person whom God will bring into your life. Having your first sexual experience together and being faithful to each other in marriage adds an extra dimension of specialness to your relationship. What a priceless wedding gift to exchange.

I'm not attempting to use fear to have you make the correct decision. You know as well as I know the dangers of using sex wrongly. You've seen girls at your own school who have had to quit because they were pregnant. You've seen girls who had to resort to abortions. You've seen girls who should still be going to school but are now saddled by a child who demands their care and attention. These girls would still be having fun as girls, going to school and making exciting decisions about their future, but that possibility is probably gone forever. I know you're aware of these things, so it's unnecessary for me to go into detail.

So, how does God intend you to use sex? Certainly He doesn't expect sex to be used to attain popularity. You should never try to buy popularity or respect. If you're able to buy it, the opinion of that person from whom you receive it is not worth much. Popularity is built upon achievement; as a result of your achievement and interests, you're respected, and as a result of respect, you become popular.

It's tragic to see a young girl giving sexual favors in an attempt to become popular. As a principal of a school, I hear frequent talk among boys about certain girls who try to gain popularity by allowing the boys to use them sexually. They kiss, they hug, they pet, and have sexual intercourse with many different boys. How degrading! Even the boys who use them talk about them like pieces of material, rather than priceless human beings. They compare their stories, and the girls in question become the scourges of the marketplace. I've often thought that if these girls could just once hear how they were discussed in the boys' locker room, they would change their attitudes and never again try to buy popularity with sex.

There will soon come a time when you feel you are in love. I will never try to minimize this, for I know how many times I thought I was in love during my teenage years. When my dad said it was puppy love, I was angry, because I was sure it was the real thing. I found out later that he was right; yet even puppy love is important.

What should you do when you think you love a boy or when you are very fond of him? Depending upon the degree of your fondness, I'm sure you will engage in some kissing and hugging and hand holding. As time progresses and your relationship becomes more intense, you may desire more physical contact. This progression is natural, and very few couples will refrain from all contact. But I caution you to take your time before you rush into these expressions of love. Time is ever so important.

A teenage girl gets caught in a trap. She hears words of love from her boyfriend and, being emotionally susceptible, she becomes vulnerable to romance and falls into the trap of believing his words of love justify her actions. She assumes that her intensity of feeling is felt as deeply by her boyfriend, yet frequently that is not the case. More often than not, what she feels is a lasting commitment, he views as a fling.

You see, many boys possess a different psychological make-up. They can engage in heavy physical contact and sex without real love or commitment. A boy often finds himself sexually excited about any girl, not just you in particular. He then looks for sexual relief, and it's not important who the girl is; if he can have sex, he will. This double standard permits him to make love without involvement. The girl who gives herself is often devastated when she discovers her beau wanted sex, not her. If you refuse to give yourself, and as a re-sult the boy breaks off the relationship, you know he needed sex, not you.

I'm not saying that all boys are like this, but many psycho-logical studies and polls have been completed which indicate that most girls who have sex have a much deeper commitment to the relationship than do the boys.

There's a joke about fathers who say to their son, "Have a good time, son, but don't bring her home." Be aware that girls who are loose stand to lose. They will be used by many people and may believe they're popular, but will usually find them-selves shelved by boys they thought were in love with them, as they go to other girls who have not been free with sex. They want something special.

Some boys effectively use the line, "If you really loved me, you would do anything for me, even have sex with me." Be aware, my dear, that if he really loved you, a boy would gladly wait until you're married for you to give yourself physi-cally to him.

Only you will be able to determine what is correct at any stage in your relationship. Ernest Hemingway in his work *Eth-ical Manifesto* said, "What's moral is what you feel good after. What's immoral is what you feel bad after." Remember, it is a girl's task not to allow herself to be used as a tool or a play-thing. This cheapens and degrades her as a person. Remem-ber, God intends for sex to be enjoyable. If He didn't He wouldn't have made a provision for it, but God also intends the ultimate sexual experience of becoming one through sex-ual intercourse to be reserved for marriage.

Many people in today's culture and society openly talk about having sex even though they're not married. They pro-pose living together to see whether or not they're compatible; they propose having sex together to see whether or not it works well for them. Don't be taken in by these arguments, my dear.

If God causes two people to become interested in each other and they fall in love and are married, He will also make the sex experience beautiful for them. Rely on Him and believe Him. Remember, He ordained the institution of marriage and made sex to be a pleasurable experience. When two people are married and grow together, and their love deepens, the sexual experience actually becomes more and more pleasurable.

As you find God's special person and fall in love, on your wedding night it will be a great thrill to be able to share with him that experience of physical intimacy that you've not shared with any other person. It's a unique gift that you alone can give to each other.

Remember, sweetheart, whenever you have questions or concerns about sex, I hope that you'll feel free to discuss them with your mother or me, for this subject is not taboo. A sex discussion is as normal and healthy as vitamins and minerals and is as real as homework or planning your future.

I have every confidence that you'll be able to handle this facet of your life in a wise and prudent way, so it will be constructive, not destructive.

Love,
YOUR FATHER

Dear Daddy:
Thank you for this chapter. I really don't feel I can add anything, but am glad you felt free to openly discuss this topic.

One thing does bother me, however. Recently, you have restricted me from participating in activities with a certain friend. When I questioned you about your reasons, you replied by telling me that you knew she had been sexually involved with an older man. I was honestly very shocked at your reason. I found it hard to believe that you'd judge someone by that standard. You acted as if you believed we spent our time together sitting around having a detailed discussion of her sexual experience. Please understand that she in no way influences my sexual standards. I have been raised in a home with healthy attitudes toward sex, and nothing anyone can say or do will change my attitudes formed over seventeen years. Thank you for showing enough concern for me to want me to carefully select my friends, but please don't worry. Remember, to God her sex sin is equal with my past lies or stealing a piece of candy. Please don't feel that one mistake makes her any less a person. I like her very much.

Hemingway's statement makes a lot of sense to me, and I'll remember it. Thank you for letting me know that you're concerned about every aspect of my life.

Love,
DAWN

What'll You Have?
Booze, Drugs, Smoking, Profanity

Dear Dawn:

I've always considered the weakest excuse for partaking in any activity to be the fact that others are doing it. I often hear teenagers at school say, "My dad drinks alcohol, and that's worse than pot, so I smoke pot. At least that doesn't hurt me." I hear other teenagers saying, "Everybody else is doing it, so why shouldn't I?"

When I hear these feeble excuses, I'm always tempted to say, "Yes, friend, it's okay if they choose to ruin their lives and their bodies, but make your decision based upon what those substances will do to your mind and your body, not theirs. They may already be 'over the hill,' but you have your whole life in front of you."

I'd like to be able to say any decision you make would affect you and you alone, but that's not usually the case. Some people who began drinking at an early age are now confirmed alcoholics, and their problem has affected many people along the way. Their parents were heartbroken; their friends were disappointed; and their marriage is currently in a state of disrepair, affecting their spouses and the lives of their children. As you can see, the consequences are usually more widespread than we'd like to admit.

When a person overindulges in any potentially harmful substance, he's saying something about his life. His actions shout out, "My life is so miserable I feel it's necessary to dull my senses in order to make it more bearable." That's pretty sad, isn't it?

You have your entire life in front of you. If you're going to get the most out of life, it's important to keep your mind alert and creative.

Many articles indicate that ingesting alcohol and other substances into your system, even in small quantities, does kill some brain cells. Why not keep yourself entirely intact, allowing you to reach your full potential?

It's always been interesting to watch young people as they smoke. They attempt to look so suave and debonair, while all the time each puff takes them deeper into the trap. The average teenager starts smoking to prove he's a man; then thirty years later tries to quit to prove the same thing.

Last week a girl in my office was talking about her drug problem. When I asked her why she used drugs, she was quick to admit that she used them because her life was very dull and because she had problems which drugs helped her temporarily forget. I asked her if she would honestly respond to one question. She nodded affirmatively, so I asked, "After you take drugs in order to forget a problem, how do those problems appear when the drugs wear off?" She replied without hesitation, "The problems seem more complicated and frightening than before I took the drugs." How revealing.

A growing problem among teenagers is that of swearing and using abusive language. I confer with several parents a week because of the language their son or daughter used at school.

There are four reasons I know of for swearing. One reason is that swearing becomes a habit. The youngster who swears frequently soon doesn't even know that he's swearing. Some swear to show that they're tough, that they can handle anything, and are one of the gang. Some kids are simply short of

vocabulary. Believe it or not, they have a hard time putting together an entire sentence if they can't put a profane word in
the middle of it. Finally, many teenagers swear to impress
others. It's interesting to note, however, that they can refrain
from swearing if need be. They can swear all day at school, yet
turn it off when they walk in the back door of the house. They
turn it off when they meet a preacher or a person from the
local church. Most of the time, they turn it off when they walk
into the classroom; so it's obvious that, if they desired to, they
could refrain from swearing all the time.

I truly believe that you'll never have a problem with drugs,
alcohol, smoking, or profanity, because I believe you think too
highly of yourself and your potential. You know that God
made you, that He's given you a delicate and intricate body
with which you can enjoy life and accomplish many things.
You realize, as I, that it's important to keep that body in the
best condition possible and not introduce into it elements
which do not belong.

Remember, above all things, that because you're a child of
His, your body is a temple for His Holy Spirit. I'm sure that
you, as I, want to make your body a temple and not a cottage.
We want the best possible housing for the Holy Spirit.

Your life will be exciting, for God has said, "I have come
that you might have life and that you might have it more
abundantly" (*see* John 10:10). An abundant life does not require alcohol, tobacco, narcotics, or vulgar or profane language. Keep clean, my dear; God will honor that, for He has
promised.

Love,
DAD

Daddy,

It is very hard for me to write about this subject. Although my involvement in these areas has been mild, compared to the majority, I feel I've disappointed you once when I experimented.

I've observed how many high-school students flow with the crowd; they don't seem to realize that it takes more strength and shows more character to stand up for what is right. Perhaps it is laziness that causes people to turn to what's suggested by the group; for saying, "No," and defending your position, require effort.

My own experience with alcohol was a result of peer pressure. I'll admit, I must have made quite an appearance holding my nose to take a sip of bourbon. I now recognize it was wrong, but that experience provided beneficial aspects as well. Through it, I realized alcohol wasn't all it's cracked up to be and that I was somewhat subject to peer pressure.

I sometimes lapse into the profanity problem as well. After hearing an almost constant flow of it daily, it's easy to let a word slip out when anger or disappointment builds up. Sometimes my profanity results from a lack of control and at other times from not thinking before I express my displeasure.

Some psychologists say that swearing is a healthy way to "blow off steam," yet I don't want to offend others, and I know, as a Christian, I should attempt to avoid using these words.

I have no desire to involve myself in smoking pot or cigarettes or using drugs. The prospective dangers present in these activities make them a stupid choice for anyone.

Please pray that I'll have the presence of mind to ask myself, "Would Jesus Christ do that?" before partaking in something that may harm myself or others. God has cleansed me for

these past activities, and now I'm asking for your forgiveness
and continued guidance in these areas.

Love,
DAWN

Don't copy the behavior and customs of this world, but
be a new and different person with a fresh newness in all
you do and think. Then you will learn from your own experience how his ways will really satisfy you.

Romans 12:2

Anger: "Boy, Was I Mad!"

Dear Dawn:

Although we are instructed to ". . . live peaceably with all men" (Romans 12:18, KJV), I've never been privileged to know a person who upon occasion wasn't subject to anger. All anger is not wrong, for we are told to "Be angry and sin not" (*see* Ephesians 4:26). Jesus Himself was angered at those who misused His Father's house. He physically removed them and their wares from the temple.

You girls have demonstrated anger from time to time, which confirmed the fact you're as normal as your dad. Anger provides a necessary outlet, on occasion, which lessens this detrimental effect upon us: Those who never "pop their corks" must pay a high internal price. I'm pleased that your anger usually subsides rather quickly, and this is often accompanied by an apology to the person it was directed against.

When you're angry, your ability to see a situation clearly and make a good decision is greatly decreased. The old adage about counting to ten before acting, when angry, is sound, although ten may not do the trick. Cooling down before taking action when one is a victim of anger will prevent many serious problems.

Anger becomes sinful when we dwell on it and calculate a way by which we can do the responsible person some harm. As we harbor anger and don't take the necessary steps to eliminate it, we alone pay the price. Both our mental and physical health are negatively affected until we clear our accounts.

We most frequently strike out in anger when we're frustrated, tired, embarrassed, nervous, feel inferior, or have sensed rejection. Anger dissolves in direct proportion to the self-respect we gain.

As Christians, our anger is often accompanied by guilt, for we know our Saviour encourages us to be slow to anger, patient, and understanding.

You'll experience anger many times, and sometimes you may feel the anger is justified, because you know you're right. In spite of the belief that you may be right, try to avoid letting anger ruin a relationship.

When anger does temporarily disrupt a relationship, isn't it great to restore that relationship to wholeness? You may accomplish this in several ways. Since you are a Christian, pray about your tendency to get angry. The Lord can and will make you more tolerant and slower to get angry. Go to the other involved person and seek his or her forgiveness or offer your forgiveness in love. Remember, God has offered to forgive you in proportion to your willingness to forgive others. Recognize that God allows us to experience anger and other emotions in order to teach us to be patient.

Thanks, God, for my daughter and the full set of emotions You've privileged her to have. Thanks for her occasional anger, that through it You may teach us both patience and Your methods of control.

Love,
DAD

Dear Daddy:
You can be sure I have a full set of emotions. Walk down the hall and look at the door I put my bare foot through! I've

never thought to thank God for my anger. I've always considered it a curse, not a blessing.

When a situation confronts me, there is always a split second in which I must decide which way to react. My problem is that I almost always choose to seek my temporary revenge and later reap the consequences. I must learn to look at the long-range effects before acting in anger.

Like Jesus in the temple, I feel some anger is very legitimate. Right now I am furious at a friend who is shirking her responsibility to an entire group. Failing to keep her commitment is not only hurting her, but all the other members involved. I feel obliged to discuss this with her. Pray that although I am angry, I'll express my concerns in love, and sin not.

On the other hand, the majority of my anger is unexcused, yet I must admit to it. This is the kind of anger I experience with my sisters, Denise and Danelle. I must learn to remember that we're on the same team, and when I physically strike out at them, I'm injuring my own teammates.

I'm glad Jesus gave us an example of anger without sin. Although I'd like to say I've learned to handle anger correctly, I can't make that claim. It's great to know, however, that when I blow it, He lets me know and stands ready to forgive me for my shortcomings, and wipes the slate clean when I confess my failings to Him. I'm glad my anger can't break or strain my relationship with Him or keep Him from loving me.

Love,
DAWN

Criticism

Dear Dawn:

It's very hard for me to accept criticism, for I often take it to mean, "You're no good."

Even last week, as I was wallpapering our bathroom, I became edgy when Mom came to inspect. "It's not done yet, dear. I haven't finished smoothing it. When it dries it becomes tighter." These were all explanations I offered before Mom could even speak. By beating her to the punch, I had hoped to eliminate any criticism she might have planned to offer. Unfortunately, when I chose this behavior, I actually curtailed suggestions which may have proven helpful and improved my performance.

I demonstrate my insecurity whenever I employ tactics to prevent criticism. Are all those people really out to get me and put me down, or is there a chance that some of them could actually be offering criticism for my benefit? Maybe I'd be shocked to find that the only true friends I had were those who cared enough to share a suggestion, even though it meant possible rejection.

As a dad, I often reject your criticism by rationalizing, "How can she have enough experience to offer criticism to me?" yet I expect you to readily accept my criticism of you, your activities, or your mode of operation. How unfair of me.

As your dad, I will never fail to offer constructive criticism, for that is my responsibility. I will, however, attempt to be more open to signals you're sending which offer critiques of my performance.

Much of growth is dependent upon our being able to accept criticism and adjust our behavior, based upon that criticism. An employer will soon observe your performance. As his evaluation reveals that you could improve your production by making some changes, he will offer constructive criticism. The attitude with which you accept his suggestions, and the adaptability you exhibit in correcting the deficiencies, may well determine your future advancement within the company.

When you turn your back on those who offer criticism and refuse to acknowledge, "They may have a point," you declare to all around that you have the ultimate answers. Such an attitude of cockiness will end many relationships and also cause those who could help to shy away, thus reducing your chances of growth.

You have a difficult time accepting criticism, just like me. Many a time I've made what I thought were excellent suggestions to help you, only to have you turn me off. After going your own way and confronting problems, you then returned and said, "I should have listened, Dad. I'm sorry." That's what makes our relationship so special. We feel the freedom to come back to each other when we've been wrong and ask, "What was that you were trying to tell me?" Let's attempt to grow together in this area of accepting criticism.

Each time I read God's Word, the Holy Spirit convicts me (or criticizes some aspect of my life), for God declares that's one of the purposes of the Bible, when He says: "The whole Bible . . . is useful to teach us what is true and to make us realize what is wrong in our lives; it straightens us out and helps us do what is right" (2 Timothy 3:16).

If we're open to God and open to people and listen to both, God will direct us concerning the changes necessary in our lives so that we may receive fulfillment and grow in a positive direction.

Remember, Dawn, criticism should not be viewed as a denouncement of you as a person, but as a chance to grow.

Love,
DADDY

P.S. "Dear, about the wallpaper in the bathroom. . . ."

Dear Daddy:

Accepting criticism is one of the hardest things for me. The words, "I have a right to correct you. Remember I am your parent" are often directed to me around our house. In almost every case, though, this statement is legitimate. I just have a terrible time accepting even friendly suggestions, from you or anyone else. The reason I feel this way is that I interpret the criticism as a put-down of myself, not as a recommendation for improving my work or making me a more effective person.

Recently, someone gave you some advice regarding my writing style. When you shared that information with me, I reacted rather harshly, by saying, "Why don't I forget the whole thing?" I now realize that even if I disagreed with his criticism, I should be thankful that he was concerned enough to offer a suggestion. The biggest put-down of all would be to have a person not even care enough to respond.

I feel somewhat edgy about criticizing you. Thank you for offering me that freedom, though. If I ever do have some advice, it will be submitted with respect, I assure you.

Without constructive criticism, the rate at which any of us grows intellectually and emotionally would decrease. I hope I'll remember that the next time you present me with some "helpful hints."

Love,
DAWN

Discouragement and Depression

Dear Dawn:

When I look at how some people live, I fully understand why they're discouraged.

On the other hand, consider the following: I have a healthy, beautiful wife; three healthy, lovely (don't let it go to your head) daughters; a large attractive home on an acre by a lake; two cars; am a member of an outstanding church; have loads of friends; have a responsible position in education; and still I get discouraged and depressed.

All people travel through peaks and valleys, and no one is exempt from periodic discouragement. When these times occur, I usually know the reason, yet occasionally I'm discouraged and don't even know the reason why. When I know the reason, I focus my attention and efforts on the problem or troubling situation, and soon discouragement flees.

My friend's daughter has a more serious problem. She is victimized by clinical depression, often lying on her bed and staring at the ceiling for a day or two. The depression can become so deep that she would be in danger of starving if no one discovered her in time to feed her. Suicide becomes a real concern in cases like hers. This is an extreme, and one which, thankfully, very few people ever have to experience.

When you share your discouragement, I've sometimes said, "That's silly. You've got so much going for you." Forgive me for this insensitive response, for when you tell me you're discouraged, I know it's ever so real to you.

Let me offer these few observations concerning discouragement and depression. Your discouragement and depression are not usually a punishment of God due to your wrongdoings. Although you can be depressed as a result of sin, most discouragement is unrelated to God, and He, above all, doesn't want us discouraged. Ride out your depression as best you can, resting assured that it is not unique to you and will soon pass. Others are experiencing discouragement as well. If you dwell on your depression and how miserable you are, the period of depression will usually be prolonged. By all means, don't do anything rash or make any important decisions when in a state of depression. When depressed, it often helps to talk to a trusted friend. If the depression continues for an extended period, counseling may be necessary.

When I'm depressed, following God's prescription seems to lift me up in the shortest amount of time. He says: ". . . Fix your thoughts on what is true and good and right. Think about things that are pure and lovely, and dwell on the fine, good things in others. Think about all you can praise God for and be glad about" (Philippians 4:8).

Dawn, you'll be discouraged and depressed from time to time, but be reminded that you have your mom and dad to share that discouragement with, and the ever-present Holy Spirit to shorten the trek through the valleys.

Lovingly,
DAD

Dear Daddy:

What perfect timing! For the past couple of days I have been trying to rid myself of this terrible depression. Your (or rather God's) advice about focusing on what is true and good might prove to be the answer to my dilemma.

I've noticed that discouragement usually sets in when I concentrate on things associated with this world so much that I lose proper perspective of my possibilities in Christ. Then I usually feel too inadequate and insecure to deal with my problems, which creates more turmoil and solves nothing. Thus, depression becomes a vicious circle.

Everyone faces depression. But I'm glad God offers to us a release. Proverbs 16:20 tells us, ". . . happy the man who puts his trust in the Lord." Please pray that I'll claim that promise and draw upon His happiness, for I do have my trust in Him.

Love,
DAWN

Entertainment

Dear Dawn:

We frequently talk about the long hours your mom and I work in order to support our family. Did you know people are now talking about a three- or four-day work week in the near future? By the time you're trained and working, you will have much more leisure time than we have ever had. How are you going to use that time? Can you imagine the amount of free time this will give you for entertainment or activities of your choice?

Even now, as I see you going to school, I observe patterns developing as to your favorite ways of spending your free time. Some of your choices please me, but I become concerned when I observe much time devoted to watching television. Although some quality programs merit your attention, the vast majority will contribute nothing to your life and, worse than that, will even prevent you from participating in worthwhile activities.

Researchers have stated we use only a very small portion of our brain power, because few of us, if any, really tax ourselves with creative or worthwhile pursuits. While our use of leisure time should be enjoyable, I believe we can find great enjoyment in taxing ourselves and our minds in interesting pursuits. Notice I said "taxing ourselves." Too many of us have gotten to be spectators and spend too much energy sitting in front of the TV. Although it may be enjoyable, we're not participating, and we are therefore only minimally involved and stimulated. Too much spectatorism leads to stagnation, and few, if any, people are attracted to a stagnant person.

Your mind offers limitless possibilities when you explore the creative potential which God has given you. You'll discover new interests, and each one will offer entertainment and fulfillment. Many people my age deteriorate in front of the television, as their physical bodies and their minds atrophy due to lack of use and infrequent challenges.

Be selective in your activities. If an activity adds to your life, pursue it. If it offers no challenge, be careful. Don't let it become a habit which consumes time yet fails to enrich your life. I got into a rut a few years ago when I spent most of my free time watching sporting events. I soon discovered how uninteresting I was. If the people I was with didn't talk about sports, I had nothing to say.

Even when work demands that you focus your talents and most of your time and attention in one area—the pursuit of job advancement—use your remaining free time in interesting and different ways. Right now you're exciting to be with, because of your multitude of interests. Please stay that way.

In a recent census taken among a large number of teenagers, the item of most importance to them was popularity. Popularity is stimulated by having a variety of interests so that your personality appeals to many people.

As I talk with parents each day, I become acutely aware that I'm not thankful enough for the excellent choices you've made in regard to entertainment and activity options. As they share heartaches resulting from their children's poor choices, I count my blessings.

Because of this, Jesus promised you satisfaction when He said: "Don't copy the behavior and customs of this world, but

be a new and different person with a fresh newness in all you
do and think. Then you will learn from your own experience
how his ways will really satisfy you" (Romans 12:2).

I hope your newness, freshness, and differences have been
as satisfying to you as they have been to me.

Love,
DADDY

Dear Daddy:

Since you've brought up this subject, I've just now realized
how much time I spend in front of the television set. I'll even
avoid church meetings or tennis matches to watch a half hour
of "Mork and Mindy." I've got to control my intake of TV, not
let it control me!

Recently, I've seen how the majority of high-school students
spend their leisure time. I frequently hear, "What parties are
going on tonight?" "Who's bringing the booze?" Many parents don't know that their children's lives center around these
activities. Because I know this, it sometimes upsets me when
you're frustrated with me and confront me with: "What have I
done wrong?" I don't mean to brag, but if you only knew the
quality children you have brought up, in comparison to the majority, you'd be pleased. If I participated in many of the activities I've been invited to, you'd have a right to be concerned.

While you're challenging me to use my leisure time in
worthwhile activities, please don't forget that sometimes I
really need time to just relax. All of us need this renewing
experience.

In the meantime, though, I'll continue taxing my mind to
broaden my interests and increase my fulfillment.

Love,
DAWN

Fitness, Not Fatness

Dear Dawn:

If I thought it would help, and I could enforce it, I'd make you sign a contract today to eat right and exercise regularly the rest of your life.

Why? Because fitness says, "I'm important and I know it. There are contributions to life that only I can make, because I'm unique." Fatness says, "I really don't think I matter. I'm not important. No one would miss me if I were gone."

Medically it is a proven fact that if you eat right and watch your weight and exercise regularly, you are very apt to have a longer life.

Most people can control their weight and their fitness. Sure, I'm aware that there are people with physical problems and glandular disorders who have no control over their weight, and my heart goes out to these people. However, it appears that you are very sound physically, so you can control this aspect of your life.

When we control our weight and our fitness, we show that we are accepting the responsibility for ourselves, for when we control weight and stay fit we are more alert and able to think more clearly and use our minds to their fullest capacity.

When we're physically fit we can vigorously enjoy activities without their taking a toll upon the organs of our body. Don't you feel sorry for people who can hardly walk up a flight of stairs without huffin' and puffin'?

Keeping yourself fit also demonstrates that you recognize your responsibility to others. If you stay fit you're going to be around to enjoy your mate a longer time. You're also going to be able to romp with your kids and do things with them that you wouldn't be able to enjoy if you were fat and dumpy and out of shape.

Keeping fit attests that we recognize our responsibility to God. As children of His, we can hardly be an example to others when we're fat and dumpy. Being fit will provide many opportunities to witness for Christ. The Word of God explains that the Holy Spirit dwells within us. This truth should provide all the fitness motivation we need, for we do want the Holy Spirit to dwell in the best of all possible temples, don't we?

We can do everything better when we are fit. Develop good habits now, while you're young, and chances are you won't be fighting these problems the rest of your life. If I had an opportunity to do it all over, I would develop a regular exercise routine and establish excellent eating habits at an early age and follow these my entire life.

When you're having a problem with fitness or diet, commit that problem to Christ, for He has promised to give you the help that is needed to allow you to control this aspect of your life. He has also promised assistance with disciplining ourselves and indicates that although discipline is not fun, the final results are very rewarding.

So, Dawn, work at it, show that you believe you are important, that others are important, and that above all God is important, by maintaining yourself at the peak of fitness.

God bless you as you work on this aspect of your life.

Love,
DAD

Dear Daddy:

I stumbled upon this chapter shortly after inhaling six molasses donuts. From those few moments of ecstasy I gained a stomachache and about 640 calories.

Although my eating habits don't normally follow this pattern, I do find that correct eating habits make me feel and look better. It amazes me that I still "punish" myself by bad eating habits, when I know the consequences.

I have never had a serious weight problem. I believe I can blame this on my self-consciousness. I care enough about my appearance that it is important to me to look as attractive as possible.

I somewhat disagree with your statement ". . . we can hardly be an example to others when we're fat and dumpy." It may be more difficult to be accepted by others, but God can work through an overweight person just as effectively as through a fit one. I'd hate to see the fatties shelved.

As long as I am capable, I'll make sure the Holy Spirit is well housed. After all, who wants a temple with crumbling walls?

Love,
DAWN AND HER DONUTS

Loneliness

Dear Dawn:

I'm certain you've already experienced loneliness. Everybody has. Few feelings are more hopeless than believing you're all alone, without a friend or ally in the world—someone who understands your present situation.

As you pass through your teen years, it will become obvious that you can be lonely whether you're by yourself or in the center of activity.

At times choosing the right course of action may be responsible for your lonely feeling. When you hold fast to your beliefs and refuse to be pressured into doing something you believe is wrong, you may find yourself standing alone. While standing alone, you may question whether the right path was worth the discomfort. Let me assure you: It was. Your action has both pleased God and made you a better person, for He has instructed you to "not be conformed to this world," (*see* Romans 12:2) and further states, "Love not the world, neither the things that are in the world" (1 John 2:15 KJV), and then commands you to "seek righteousness and the kingdom of God first" (*see* Matthew 6:33).

When you follow these instructions, God promises that all your needs will be supplied (*see* Philippians 4:19) and among your needs are comfort and the potential of freedom from loneliness. Jesus has promised that He would provide strength for every situation, and that includes standing up for what you believe is correct. "I can do all things through Christ who strengthens me" (*see* Philippians 4:13).

Your loneliness will be a very temporary condition, for your stands will soon be respected by your peers. In fact, you'll find the quality of your friends rising and the numbers increasing, as others seek strength through you.

What a neat feeling to know you're really never alone once you've invited Jesus Christ into your life, for He establishes permanent residency.

When Jesus Christ walked the earth and ministered to those around Him, He sensed man's loneliness and need for comfort and fellowship. Because of His love and acute awareness of man's condition and needs, Jesus, prior to ascending into heaven, promised to send a Comforter, in the form of the Holy Spirit, to perform this ministry. How comforting it is to know that even during these lonely times when you feel everyone, including your parents, has forsaken you, He cares and dwells within you to somewhat fill the real or imagined void. You alone prevent Him from totally erasing your feelings of loneliness.

As you nurture your faith through prayer, God's Word, and fellowship, your sensitivity to the Holy Spirit grows; and, as it grows, your feelings of loneliness become less frequent and diminish in intensity. Knowing the Holy Spirit dwells within doesn't mean you'll cease to be depressed or lonely, since you still must allow Him to minister to you. You may often feel sorry for yourself and your self-pity so occupies your mind that it causes you to forget about the help He offers.

Even Jesus was wracked by loneliness just prior to His crucifixion, when all His disciples fell asleep in His most intense hour of need. Yet when He called out, God the Father answered Him, as the Holy Spirit will do for us.

But, when we don't receive assistance, it is our fault, for Jesus has promised us, "I will never leave you nor forsake you" (*see* Hebrews 13:5). He further states that He accounts for every sparrow and is much more concerned with us. I hope you feel as much comfort as I do when you read these promises.

As Christians we have another privilege. Because we know the antidote for loneliness, we have the opportunity to help others. I've been so pleased to see you paying special attention to persons who are lonely and miserable. One of my greatest thrills was receiving a letter from a teacher, which stated, "She is so sweet. She cares so deeply for other people. Today she saw a person on the playground who was all alone crying. She put her arm around her and asked to be her friend. The little girl was fine the remainder of the day." I thank God that He's made you sensitive to the needs of other people and willing to help them when they're hurting.

Just as you like to help others, we'd like to help you. Don't keep your hurt and loneliness within. Please feel free to come to your dad and mom and share your innermost feelings and loneliness. We love you and are happy when you're happy and hurt deeply when you hurt. We'll take your feelings seriously, and we'll listen and do all within our power to meet your needs. Occasional loneliness makes you no less a person in our eyes, since we, too, experience the reality of loneliness.

May your life be filled with joy and your lonely days be few. May even your lonely days be less intense as you remember His presence in your life.

Love,
DAD

Dear Daddy:

Webster's Dictionary says loneliness is the quality or state of being without company. This definition is shallow, and maybe it's untrue. As you have written, you can be in a crowded room, surrounded by friends, and still be lonely. An average of thirteen teens kill themselves each day, and I'm sure loneliness plays a major role in these suicides.

What a relief it is to know that we, as Christians, are never alone. I agree with you that we feel lonely because we don't claim God's promise that He will never leave us or forsake us. It makes me think of the following story.

One night a man had a dream. He dreamed he was walking along the beach with the Lord. Across the sky flashed scenes from his life. In each scene, he noticed two sets of footprints in the sand. One belonged to him and one to the Lord. When the last scene had flashed before him, he looked back at the footprints and noticed that for many miles along the path there was only one set of footprints in the sand. He also noticed that this happened during the lowest and saddest times of his life. This really bothered him, and he questioned the Lord. "Lord, You said that once I decided to follow You, You would walk all the way with me, but I noticed that during the most troublesome times of my life, there was only one set of footprints. I don't understand it. When I needed You the most, You deserted me."

The Lord replied, "My precious, precious child. I love you. During the times of trial and suffering, when you see only one set of footprints, it was then that I carried you."

When we experience loneliness, we look too hard for those footprints. Pray that I'll realize and take to heart the promise He gives: "I will *never, never* fail you nor forsake you" (*see* Hebrews 13:5).

Love,
DAWN

Worry

Dear Dawn:

The most fruitless waste of time is worrying. When we worry, we use up vital energy which could otherwise be used for productive purposes. It's easy to say, "Don't worry," yet that's very difficult to put into practice.

As you mature and assume increased responsibilities, there seem to be more and more situations which you cannot control. When you can't control a situation or affect its outcome, you tend to worry about it. When you worry the results can be disastrous. You become ineffective in your present situation, you begin to question your capabilities and worth, and your physical and mental health deteriorate.

I'm often surprised when one of my seemingly calm friends suddenly is diagnosed as having ulcers. It reinforces the fact that appearances are deceiving, and those we set up as models of calmness and describe as worry free are actually being eaten up, internally, through worry.

It's normal to be nervous from time to time. New experiences, speaking in public, the big game, your final examination, and the important date all cause a certain amount of nervousness, yet worry goes beyond nervousness and usually entails deeper concern, over a longer period of time.

Worrying has been described as "interest paid on trouble before it's due." How true. Our minds are vitally involved in worrying as they focus upon the anticipated event and envision all that could go wrong with the coming situation. As anxiety and worry build, they are translated to our bodies in the form of headaches, stomachaches, diarrhea, and many other physical symptoms.

Next comes the outgrowth of the symptoms, as fingernails are bitten to the core, nervous pacing back and forth occurs, and beads of sweat rise to the surface of the skin. The event you were fretting about comes and goes without any of the anticipated calamities occurring. You sigh and say, "How silly I was to worry." Yet, next time, you repeat the same folly.

Jesus Christ talked about worry and commanded us to not worry about our lives, our food, our drink, our clothing, for His Father takes care of the sparrows, and if He does this, surely He will take better care of us, His prized possessions.

He asks the vital question, "Will all your worries add a single moment to your life?" then assures you that He will give you what you need if you give Him first place in your life and live as He wants you to.

Much of our worry occurs when we think too far ahead, yet Jesus offers a cure for this when He says, "So don't be anxious about tomorrow. God will take care of your tomorrow too. Live one day at a time" (Matthew 6:34).

Listen, Dawn, when worry seems to have you cornered, I offer the advice I've found so helpful:

1. Ask yourself, "What is the worst possible thing which could occur in the situation I'm now worrying about?" Usually the answer will reveal that you're much, much more concerned than the situation warrants.

2. Read Matthew 6:25–34 and claim the promises of Jesus.

You're in good hands.

Love,
DAD

Dear Daddy:

I was once described by an older friend as being the first eighth grader he knew who would develop ulcers prior to high-school graduation. Right now, I'm so nervous about an upcoming project that I have a sick stomach and am actually shaking. The worst thing is that I know worrying will hurt me, not help me; yet it's become as natural as eating, and I feel I just can't help but do it.

I know the Bible says all the worry in the world can't add one day to my life, yet I need your prayers that I may use God's promises and power to control my fears and curb my worrying.

Worrying, I feel, is caused by examining ourselves and focusing too much on our own problems. In my case, I begin thinking, "I'm going to fail when I try, and then what will all these people think of me?" When that happens, it becomes easy to blow my faults and past failures way out of proportion.

I know when this occurs, I need to sit down and get everything back into perspective: God's perspective.

Although He says, "Cast your care upon Him for He careth for you" (*see* 1 Peter 5:7), I so much need your prayers that I'll be able to take His advice and my own understanding and put them to work, living one day at a time.

Thanks for having so much confidence in me.

Love,
DAWN

Communication

Dear Dawn:

You've probably thought everything you said to others was understood. I felt the same way, until a short time ago, when I read some recent research which revealed that when we communicate, only 7 percent of our message comes from the words we speak.

If that's true, 93 percent of our message is conveyed by other means, which often overrule our words. This same research further stated that 55 percent of our message comes through nonverbal means, and the other 38 percent of our message is sent by the tone of our voices.

I'm glad I know this. Its effects are far-reaching, since I do want people to understand what I'm really saying. Don't you?

I may speak and tell you, "I'm willing to openly listen to your explanation," yet proceed to roll my eyes back into my head and sigh with each statement you make, letting you know I'm really not interested in listening at all. You may openly declare your willingness to do the dishes for Mom, yet the tone of your voice really says, "I'll do them all right, but I hate you for making me do them." We could all profit from being more aware of the messages we send.

When I correct you for not having the proper attitude, slamming an object down in disgust, or gruffly responding to your sisters or me, I am doing so because you are conveying a

80   *Dear Dawn, Dear Dad*

message which I don't believe you really mean. You're approaching the age where soon most of the messages you send will take place outside the friendly confines of the family. By saying one thing to people and sending another message, others will begin to question your honesty, and this will affect the quality of your relationship. My corrections are also intended to keep you from falling into the habit of unconsciously sending negative messages to those around you.

I'm happy for your positiveness, and for the good messages you normally convey, for they carry with them love and understanding. How important to realize that a look, a smile, a touch, or a hug, often sends a message which far exceeds a host of words.

As a Christian, the most important message you can give to others is one of love, concern, and understanding. If, as you talk to others, they sense love, warmth, and concern in your actions and tones, honesty will be added to your words; and soon they, too, may share the faith in your Saviour.

You've often told me you love me, and I've told you the same, and for the most part our actions and tones have verified that love. Let's ask God to keep us ever aware that we owe honesty of communication to all we meet, and that will only be accomplished when our actions, and the tones of our voices, support the claim of our words. A familiar chorus says it so well.

> What you are speaks so loud
> The world can't hear what you say,
> They're looking at your walk
> Not listening to your talk
> They're judging by your actions
>   everyday.

> Don't believe that you'll deceive
> by claiming that you've never known
> They'll accept what they see
> And know you to be
> They'll judge by your life alone.

Dawn, be careful of what you say, and let your actions and the tone of your voice add honesty to your words.

Love,
DAD

Dear Daddy:

I can't believe those statistics! To think that only 7 percent of what we say is effectively communicated is pretty frightening. Now I realize how important it is that I'm corrected with statements like, "Take that look off your face," or, "Lower the tone of your voice."

The last part of your chapter deals with a problem I often observe. So many people profess to be Christians, yet so few of us act like it. In doing so, we not only hurt ourselves and disappoint God, but also discourage others. Several times I've heard, "If that's what it's like to be a Christian, I don't need it." If someone doesn't intend to live a Christian life, he should at least have the courtesy to leave its reputation intact by not claiming the name.

Recently, one of my friends, after telling me that she was a Christian, proceeded to relate to me how "bombed" she got that evening she arrived on Catalina. I wonder if she would have done the same thing if she had known she was in the presence of a non-Christian. I believe we'd be astounded if we knew the extent to which we, through our words or actions, negatively affect those around us.

All Christians must realize that the memorized verses we can spout off mean nothing unless there is the "something different" that distinguishes us from the crowd. Communication, physically as well as verbally, is an essential life function. Thanks for the special insight you've given in this area.

Love,
DAWN

Contentment

Dear Dawn:

It's difficult for me to write about an area in which I consider myself deficient. You've seen and heard me scheme to change jobs, make more money, move to a better area, change churches, and effect many other changes which certainly have demonstrated: "Your dad's not always content." Even though we have a lovely home, car, and all the material things we need, I'm still always reaching out for more.

Secretly I know, however, even if we had more, contentment will not come until the Lord changes my spirit and attitude. I pray that He will allow me to truly become content. I'm confident that contentment can be obtained, for Paul learned to be content in whatever state he found himself. How beautiful it would be to be able to claim that statement with Paul. Contentment comes from within and is a gift from God. Ideally, it should not be dependent upon outward circumstances.

I tend to separate my life into categories, then claim contentment in certain areas but discontentment in others. Realistically I know that God's true contentment is capable of spanning all areas of my life.

Caution must be exercised to not use contentment as a cop-out. I've heard people piously state, "I'm content right where I am and won't apply for that promotion," although I've known the real reason for not applying was their fear that they might not get the job. I've also known people who refused advancement because they were too lazy.

I firmly believe that you cannot be truly contented unless you use to your fullest the abilities God has given you. When the Scriptures encourage us to do all unto the glory of God, we are expected to do just that: the best job possible. When we follow this scriptural direction, advancement opportunities will naturally present themselves. God expects quality from Christians and wants us to be rewarded with advancement; yet, while we're serving in our current positions, He expects our best efforts as well.

God has promised us that when we handle well the things He has given us, including material possessions, jobs, and money, He will be able to trust us with more. He's also told us that when we abide in Him, we can ask what we will, and it will be done unto us. While this sounds risky for Him, it's really not, since abiding in Him would assure that our requests would be within His will.

To be content we must realize that God has decided to place us in our present situations for His reasons. If we exhibit contentment with His decision, we are a witness for Him; if we exhibit discontent, we say to others, "I'm dissatisfied with His choice." If I'm dissatisfied with His choice, it follows that I'm dissatisfied with Christ. What then do I have to offer the world around me?

I must admit that my discontent has often detracted from Christ. Only during the last two years have I begun to taste of the contentment He offers.

I trust and pray that in spite of my shortcomings in this area, the Lord will bless you with contentment in your schooling, your choice of a mate, your life's work, with your children, and most of all in your relationship with Him.

There's nothing I'd like more than to see you surpass your dad in the attainment of contentment.

Love,
DADDY

Dear Daddy:

Surprisingly, our opinions on this subject differ greatly.

I believe it can be unhealthy to be content. Many people claim satisfaction with life and all it has to offer, but because of this attitude, never reach their full potential.

God, Himself, was not content with the state of the world, so sent His Son, Jesus Christ, to offer new life to all who would invite Him into their lives. Through Him, we can observe this perfect peace and even experience it to a certain degree. But I'm convinced that contentment can never be fully reached, because we are not perfect, as Jesus is.

I thank God for the example He gave us to strive for and anxiously await the day when we, His children, will be perfectly satisfied, while we personally experience all He has to offer.

Love,
DAWN

Empathy

Dear Dawn:

I am always deeply touched when I observe you or your sisters reaching out to comfort those in need. My favorite comment appeared on one of Denise's report cards. It said, "She is such a sweet girl. She always tries to help those who are having a problem or are being picked on by others." Tonight Danelle telephoned to ask if I could get one more Bible so she could give it to her friend who's moving to another area. Dawn, your recent expressions of concern for Debbie and Casey's welfare while in college touched me.

Caring for others is a beautiful thing. It's what life is all about. What a sterile, concrete place this world would be if we didn't feel for someone and reach to help.

When you feel, then act to help, your act of kindness is actually offered to God, who has said when you help one of His, it's the same as actually helping Him. Imagine, every act of kindness you've committed not only pleased the person in need, but God as well. What a bonus! In all the accounts of Jesus, I have never read that He was too busy to assist anyone needing help. What empathy!

Forgive me, Dawn, for the times I've been too busy to patiently sit down so you could explain your need or how bad you felt about something.

We frequently take time to help others, yet fail to do so with the very people we love the most: our own family. I suppose we feel they'll love us, regardless of our actions; so we spend our energies reaching out to others. I sure regret the times I've let you down and failed to meet your needs.

I'm so proud of the soft hearts and sensitive spirits you and your sisters have toward others. You'll experience joy and fulfillment in life as you seek to help those in need. Sometimes the help will come in the form of a hug, an act of kindness, a gift of money, cleaning a house, protecting the abused, comforting the hurting, or just listening. Though the act may receive little notice from those around, be thankful, for the less thanks you receive from men, the greater reward your heavenly Father will bestow upon you in glory.

Keep reaching out to others.

Love,
DAD

Dear Daddy:

After growing up in this house, how could I help having empathy for others? You and Mom have been very good examples in this area. Recently, I've seen your sensitivity in a very tangible way. You offered to house a friend in need and accepted him as a part of our family. I, too, am proud of your soft hearts and sensitive spirits.

I react in anger when I see callous, unfeeling people. Although I sometimes get mad at myself for being too sentimental, I'd much rather be at this extreme than have little or no feelings for others.

Thank you for reminding me of the responsibility I have to my family. It's true that I sometimes hurt the people I love the most. Thanks, also, for reminding me that I receive a double benefit for an act of kindness: both my self-satisfaction and God's.

Love,
DAWN

Forgiveness

Dear Dawn:

There will be frequent occasions during your lifetime when you'll feel you've been wronged. Some of these times will be valid, and some you'll discover were misjudgments on your part.

When you're wronged you have two options. The first and most destructive is to harbor resentment in your heart and hold a grudge. I've chosen this course of action many times in my life, feeling I was truly punishing the other person, only to find out later that I was the one who was suffering. I've also seen you suffer while at odds with a friend.

Holding a grudge colors your total existence, while draping a black cloud over your life. Your performance falters, your attitude toward others sours, and in general you function at a lower than normal level. Our nation's hospitals are filled with people who've suffered physical, emotional, and mental problems as a result of their inability to forgive people.

I thank God that most of the time I see you exercising the option of forgiveness. When your friend has wronged you, I've heard you call to clear up the situation. When your sister has gotten you into trouble, then apologized, I've heard you forgive. When I've been unduly harsh, you've come running back with open arms.

Forgiveness isn't always easy. In fact, as you assume more

responsibility and someone wrongs your children or family, it may seem humanly impossible, but God will provide the means to forgive.

No human story ever gripped me more than that of Corrie ten Boom, who, through Christ, was able to forgive, love, and pray for the guard who actually contributed to her sister's death in a concentration camp.

Be reminded that your forgiveness is tied into God's forgiveness. Jesus says in Matthew 6:14, 15 (NAS): "For if you forgive men for their transgressions, your heavenly Father will also forgive you. But if you do not forgive men, then your Father will not forgive your transgressions." How important it is for us to realize that we are the key to God's forgiveness of us. We have the power to shut it off or make it a reality.

Every time you feel someone has wronged you, carefully consider the problems you create for yourself by not forgiving, then reach out, forgive, and feel the power and cleansing of Jesus flow into your life.

Sometimes you've wronged someone and failed to ask his forgiveness. When this occurs your fellowship with him and God diminishes. Jesus has instructed you to go to the person you've wronged and ask his forgiveness, and then pray for God's forgiveness also. When we don't follow His directions, we rob ourselves of joy.

Dawn, be eager to forgive and seek forgiveness, for only then can you experience the fulfillment which Jesus meant for you to have.

Love,
DAD

Dear Daddy:

A couple of months ago, you expressed a concern about my inability to forgive. Admitting I am wrong and asking for forgiveness doesn't come easily to me. I'm not sure whether or not it does for anyone else, either, but I complicate the matter by involving my ego and a great deal of pride. Thank you for pointing out this problem area and, please, continue to help me resolve it.

Accepting an apology also poses some problems for me. When I think I have been unjustly wronged, I often feel that the person who put me through such torment deserves the same and ask myself, "Why should I get him off the hook by accepting his apology?" I later realize how I've suffered by harboring this resentment.

When I can't forgive my sister because she ripped my shirt or my friend who scratched my record, pray that I will remember that Jesus Christ forgave those who crucified Him! My problems are very insignificant, and certainly not worth the turmoil, when placed in the right perspective.

Love,
DAWN

P.S. Please remember this chapter if and when I ever show you the back fender on the car.

Humor

Dear Dawn:

A sense of humor is vitally important to a fulfilled life. A person devoid of humor is, to my way of thinking, an incomplete person, for he fails to recognize and enjoy the many amusing situations which make up everyday life.

Humor adds a vital dimension to relationships. True friends can laugh with each other or at each other. Happy people are healthier people, since laughing and the release which humor provides are so vital to physical and emotional health. I thank God for your sense of humor and the times He's privileged us to "crack up" together.

As a child, Red Skelton used to do me in; now we share Steve Martin as a favorite. More important than laughing at the professional comedians, however, is the spontaneous humor which wells up within a person upon observing or participating in an amusing situation. One of my most precious memories was the New Year's party that we shared at Grandma's house in Chicago. We laughed until we cried. I can still see Grandma, unable to talk, with tears streaming down her face.

I trust you'll never lose your sense of humor, for uninterrupted seriousness would be like an indefinite prison sentence. At the same time, humor should never embarrass anyone or be used inappropriately to detract from someone's lack of effort or accomplishment.

I admit my humor is at times a little offbeat and peculiar, but I thank you for your laughs. Please accept my apologies for the times I've embarrassed you by doing an amusing dance in public, but it was my way of saying humor is really important.

I have to think that God values a sense of humor as well. I can't believe Jesus didn't know what was going on while He slept in the boat, during the storm, as the disciples panicked. I have to believe that God knew He would blow the minds of the furnace tenders when He allowed Shadrach, Meshach, and Abed-nego to walk out of the fiery furnace, unscathed. Jesus had to possess a little humor when He told Peter and his crew, who had fished all night, to pull those nets in and throw them on the other side of the boat.

When Peter, in an effort to protect Jesus, cut off the guard's ear, I sometimes wish Jesus had picked up the guard's ear and put it back on upside down, just to lend credibility to the importance of a sense of humor.

I hope you'll maintain your sense of humor throughout life, for it'll make the journey for you and everyone you encounter much more pleasant. By the way, did I tell you about the one. . . .

Love,
DAD

Dear Daddy:

I am in total agreement with the contents of this chapter. Humor enhances every relationship and is both beneficial and enjoyable to all who partake in it.

I do wish, however, that you'd learn to express your "unique" style of humor in, perhaps, a more refined manner.

Love,
DAWN

Loyalty

Dear Dawn:

Loyalty is highly prized. Employers heap praise upon employees who are team members. The most rewarding friendships are those marked by a high degree of loyalty for each other. A secure feeling exists when you know you can count on the loyalty of that other person. From a tender age, I've observed your undying loyalty to pets, friends, and us. This pleases me greatly.

Although loyalty has been important to this point in your life, it will assume even greater importance in your teen years and during your marriage. You've shared with me that your friends have become all-important at this time in your life. It's normal to want to please your peers more than your parents when you're a teenager. (After all, your parents will always be on your side, but friends come and go.) Since it is normal for teens to try to please their peers through their behavior, loyalty to them and from them amounts to an unspoken code of honor. I could literally assault some students at my school without their betraying their friends. While this trait of loyalty is admirable, it also poses some distinct problems, since many teens actually participate in wrongdoings or fail to warn their friends of pitfalls, for fear that these actions would be interpreted as disloyalty.

Being loyal should not overshadow the importance of being

honest. I've had the sad experience of talking with a heartbroken teenager, who, through his sobs stated, "He was my best friend, and I knew he was taking drugs. If only I had been honest with him and told him what I thought, he might be alive today." True loyalty involves honesty with the person to whom you're being loyal. Loyalty is one of the chief reasons for teenagers becoming involved in drugs, sex, and alcohol, which provide startling demonstrations of its misuse.

Loyalty is noble, unless it is blind, in which case it suddenly becomes a weakness. I never expect you to turn your back on what you know to be God's direction or the right course of action, just to be known as loyal.

Family loyalty is extremely important. All of us need some safe place to let our hair down with the assurance we're still accepted and loved. Many outside forces exist which create problems and pressures for family members. When they occur, the loyalty and understanding of other family members act to soothe the hurt and lessen the self-doubts. A lack of family loyalty and support in a crisis situation can be "the straw that breaks the camel's back" as the perplexed member feels all alone and forsaken.

I'm glad you've always been loyal and hope you felt my loyalty. Even when you and I disagree on an issue, or I'm disappointed in your chosen behavior, I want to be loyal.

Mom and I have talked on several occasions about your grandmother and the high degree of loyalty she possessed. Although she must have been disappointed in us children at times, we compared notes and never once heard her make a critical statement to one of us about the other. That's loyalty at its finest.

As we support each other as part of a family, each member is less apt to succumb to the pressures of outside forces.

Dawn, as Christians, we share in another facet of loyalty. Once we accept Jesus Christ as our personal Saviour, we become family members in the Body of Christ (composed of all believers). The Scriptures make us aware of the obligations we have to the members of this Body. We are to be loyal to them, love them, encourage them, forgive them, fellowship with them, strengthen them, and pray for them, only for starters.

A general truth exists: *When you're loyal to others you can expect their loyalty in return.* Nowhere is this truth more evident or important than through the words of Jesus, who said, "If you confess me before men, I will confess you before my Father in heaven" (*see* Matthew 10:32).

I'm glad you are loyal, and I trust loyalty will remain a vital part of your life.

Love,
DAD

Dear Daddy,

I agree that loyalty is a quality that should be present in every serious relationship. During my junior-high and high-school years, loyalty has had to be a part of every friendship, no matter how shallow it might be.

It's so easy to perceive loyalty to be not saying or doing anything which may contradict the wishes of your friend, but loyalty without honesty means very little.

Today I experienced an important lesson regarding loyalty, but it came in a rather negative way. My best friend, Linda, and I were in my bedroom when we discovered some old letters stashed away in a box in my closet. As we began reading many of them, I became embarrassed, for many of the letters contained statements about Linda, which I had written to other people. I felt ashamed and sorrowful about my past behavior.

As uncomfortable as this incident was, it helped me realize that disloyalty not only harms others and their reputation, but it can also deeply hurt me. Luckily, our relationship had grown to the point that the letters did not become a divisive factor.

As I was reading the Bible the other night, I came across the story of Judas and his betrayal of Jesus. My disloyalty may never be so important as to render death to an individual, but it could mean death to a relationship and deep hurt to all involved.

There is one point at which I disagree with your letter. I don't believe it is more normal for all teenagers to try to please their peers more than their parents. Maybe I'm wrong, but it gives me greater satisfaction to receive your approval than the approval of my fellow students.

Daddy, thank you for the loyalty you've shown me. A statement you made to me, quite recently, perfectly depicted that loyalty. I had been going to church every Wednesday and Thursday night for weeks, plus actively participating on Sundays. Our youth pastor had asked me to attend an all-weekend seminar in a nearby city, and I didn't feel that I would be able to do it and keep up my studies and have a little time to myself to relax before returning to school on Monday. He called me again and again, and even urged some of my friends to call to tell me they were planning to attend the seminar. The pressure and guilt were really getting to me, when I came to you and explained the situation. Your answer bolstered my spirits and made me feel so good. "Dawn, I'll support you in whatever decision you make. You know what you need at this time. Never feel guilty when you say, 'No,' for a good reason." I immediately knew you would take my side, stick by me, and even present my position, if the youth pastor called to pressure me again. Your comment of loyalty and trust was something I really needed, and I'll always remember and cherish it.

Thank you.

Love,
DAWN

Patience

Dear Dawn:

Last night we watched the Dodgers' game with 37,000 other baseball fans. Our seats happened to be in the upper deck, just as far away from home plate as one could be.

Although our vantage point for viewing the game could have been improved, it provided a perfect setting for demonstrating the importance of patience. Arriving early to down a few hot dogs (why do they always taste so much better at the ballpark?), we watched the headlights of the cars streaming into the parking lot. From high atop our vantage point, we observed cars cutting in front of each other, spurting at excessive speeds, and narrowly missing pedestrians in the crosswalk, all to gain a few seconds' advantage over one another. No one seemed to be patient.

No sooner had the Dodgers taken a three-run lead in the sixth inning, than people began to shuffle out to their cars to beat the rush. Standing for the seventh-inning stretch, we glanced to the parking lot during the last refrain of "Take Me Out to the Ballgame." By now traffic was bumper-to-bumper where each exit empties out onto the main drag. By the beginning of the ninth inning, one-third of the capacity crowd had left and, entering the last half of the ninth, two-thirds of the crowd was already in the parking lot.

All those people who had paid good money to see the game

were so impatient that they missed a large portion of the ball-game in order to be the first on the freeways.

We sat in our section, leisurely talking, until the entire stadium was almost emptied, when the ushers finally asked us to proceed toward the exit. When we reached the parking lot, some of the exits were still jammed with drivers honking at each other while cutting in and out of lines in order to gain a space or two. We sat in the parking lot, reading and talking, until all was clear, then proceeded, without traffic or anxiety, all the way home. What a beautiful lesson that provided for life.

During the process of growing up, you'll want to rush so many things. I know, for I did, and so did your mother. When some of your friends have steady dates and you don't, you'll question the fairness of it all. When friends seem to have it all together, and you feel you're still floundering, you'll even question God about why He hasn't dealt with you as swiftly and fairly. At those times, sit back and relax and let the hectic world jockey for position, knowing that your God will provide what you need, at the time most beneficial to you and Him.

Impatience is not a problem exclusive to the young, for I, too, experience it all too regularly. As I grow older, I remind God that my life is more than half gone, and I've yet to experience so much I know He has for me. As you know, I also get impatient with you and expect behavior far in advance of your age. At those times, the Lord subtly reminds me " . . . be patient with everyone" (1 Thessalonians 5:14), even your daughters.

God has said: ". . . patience develops strength of character in us and helps us trust God more each time we use it until finally our hope and faith are strong and steady" (Romans 5:4).

Dawn, my prayer for you is that you develop a strong realization of how much Jesus loves you. If this becomes a reality, you'll realize that He desires the best for your life and with His great wisdom will give you those things you believe you need now precisely at the time He chooses, based upon your ability to handle them.

So sit back in His love. Look at the crowd scramble for position, while you rest assured that ". . . he careth for you" (1 Peter 5:7 KJV).

Love,
DADDY

P.S. Be patient with Dad as well.

Daddy,

What a strange feeling it was to watch those cars from our seats. It showed that people really are continually rushing, but not enjoying life. Patience is not a part of the fruit of the Spirit that the majority of Christians utilize, although the potential is always present. I'll have to admit, though, we had a better view of the parking lot than we did of the playing field! Could you have sprung for better seats? Our hot dogs cost more than our tickets!

I've always admired the way you exercise patience. It has given me a standard to strive for, although it is apparent I often fail. Today was an excellent example. You asked me to take Danelle and Denise to get an ice-cream cake, because Grandma was joining us for dinner. After ten minutes of angrily discussing which one to choose, we finally all agreed. After returning to the display case, we all decided upon a cake—all, that is, except Denise. I, in disgust, left the store and returned to the car. I was soon followed by Denise, leaving Danelle alone to purchase her cake. On the way home, with Danelle sobbing in the backseat, I realized I had made quite a mistake. How could I have been so impatient? My failure was responsible for breaking her little heart.

Daddy, please pray that in that split second in which I decide how I'll react, I'll choose the way Christ would have. A lack of control and patience not only harms me, but can also destroy others. Right now I have to go apologize to a special little sister.

Love,
DAWN

Privacy

Dear Dawn:

All of us have a need for privacy. Some require more than others. Privacy can be obtained in a variety of ways. While some seek to physically be alone, others have mastered the art of escaping mentally, even though surrounded by a host of people.

When you were younger, privacy didn't seem important to you, for you were rarely without playmates. "The more the merrier" seemed to be your motto. Friends are becoming even more important, now that you're a teenager, yet the need for privacy has suddenly crept into the picture.

Some teens worry about their need to be alone and question, "Am I normal? Am I a loner or recluse? Is something the matter with me because I need to be by myself at times?" Let me assure you, needing to be alone is not only normal, it is healthy. A recent article called attention to the fact that those who could be contented when alone were better adjusted than those who could only achieve contentment while in the presence of others. Privacy only becomes unhealthy when used for extended periods of time to totally avoid interaction with people.

Some of my private times have been my most productive. In the confines of my study, or on my walk around the lake, I find relief from the pressures of life, while taking time to re-evaluate my goals, clarify my points of view, and dwell on the blessings that God has bestowed upon me.

I'm pleased, not offended, when I see your door shut, for I know you, too, need time for reflection and other things you deem important. Mistakenly, parents sometimes believe the need for privacy says, "I don't want to be with you," yet we know this is not the case. We respect your need for privacy and expect the same from you.

Contrary to popular belief, privacy doesn't always mean being alone, for at times privacy will include a trusted friend, a sister or brother, or your dad or mom. As you know, your dad and mom need to have privacy together, just as you need to have private moments with your trusted friends. The importance of sharing ideas and thoughts with a trusted friend or someone you love cannot be overestimated. What a comfort to discover that your friend shares similar feelings to those you're currently experiencing. Knowing this can uplift your spirits and confirm the fact that you are indeed a normal person.

As a general rule, we allow others into our private lives only when our level of trust in them reaches a certain degree. If they then disappoint us, our trust level decreases, and they are eliminated from our approved list.

I'm so pleased on those occasions when you choose to share your private thoughts and concerns with me, for it demonstrates your trust in me and the value you've placed upon my experience and judgment. Even when you can't ask my advice, I'm glad for the chance to share, for no human is more interested in your life or loves you more than I do.

As you grow older, your mom and I will share more and more with you, yet at this age we choose to withhold selected information, in an effort to protect you from undue concern or worry. Please recognize the fact that we will never withhold anything from you that we believe would be in your best interests.

As you mature and move toward independence, your private thoughts and concerns once shared with us may be shared with others outside the home, whom you trust. Ultimately, when you're married, your mate will meet your needs as your chief confidant.

While this is to be expected, please be aware we are always here and keenly interested in helping you in whatever capacity we can.

As a Christian, privacy offers a beautiful experience, for, when you're physically alone, your constant companion, the Holy Spirit, has an opportunity to minister to you.

The Scripture seems to support our need for privacy. Paul's times alone greatly added to the effectiveness of his ministry. Moses was compelled to be in the wilderness for years, so the Lord could speak to him in preparation for his leadership role with the children of Israel. Jesus Himself spent forty days and forty nights alone in the wilderness, to be tempted in every way, in order that during the difficult times we all face in our lives, we could personally relate to Him and His experiences. You and I, too, no less servants than Paul or Moses, need to be alone from time to time, so we can "be still and know that He is God" (*see* Psalms 46:10). When we take time to withdraw from the hustle and bustle of life, to reflect upon who He is, all of life falls into place.

Enjoy your privacy,
DADDY

Dear Daddy:

Sometimes I feel it's impossible to achieve any type of privacy in this house. A closed door proves to be an irresistible curiosity, and just must be opened. Soaking in a tub is always interrupted by the clanking of scissors prying at a lock. While I'm not an authority on privacy, I believe, at times, I'm an expert on the lack of it.

Privacy is essential but, unfortunately, is often considered a luxury. I'm sure everyone has experienced times when people and the problems they create become so exasperating that you feel like screaming. Our world would be more pleasant and more healthy if people took some time out of a hectic schedule and reserved it for privacy.

Please understand that when I rebel against taking a sister to the beach, shopping, or the movies, I'm not being selfish, as it may appear. I, too, need time with friends, just as you do.

I'll try to be more conscious of your needs in this area. Pray that I will realize that it's not that you don't want to be with me; it is just your desire for privacy.

Love,
DAWN

Respect Has Its Rewards

Dear Dawn:

I hailed a cab in front of San Francisco State University. As it pulled to the curb, I hopped into the front seat and, as expected, we exchanged our polite *hellos*. The driver was crude and unshaven, of foreign extraction, and new to San Francisco. He swore like a trooper, yet he had a profound impact upon my day.

As we wheeled up and down the hills of San Francisco, toward my hotel, he related an incident in which he was involved. It had occurred a week ago, and as he related the details to me, he became very emotional. I was tempted to say, "Forget the story and just mind your driving," but I was intrigued by what he was saying.

"Last week I picked up this handicapped lady. She could hardly make it in the front seat, so I went around and opened the door for her and helped her lift her leg into the cab. She was old. She was overweight. She was handicapped.

"When I got her where she wanted to go, the only place close to the sidewalk was a loading zone. As I pulled in to let her out, a policeman said, 'Hey, buddy, don't go in that loading zone, or I'll give you a ticket.' I rolled down my window and tried to explain that I had a handicapped person in the cab, and I wanted her to be able to get out on the sidewalk and not worry about the traffic. He said he didn't care, and I told him I was going to do it anyhow.

"As I pulled in the loading zone, I walked around the car and opened the door. I took time to help her get out of the cab, handed her the cane, walked her to the door, and helped her into the hallway. When I came back, the officer didn't let me drive away until he wrote the ticket.

"I was really steamed up. In fact, I went right down to the station and explained it to the officer in charge of the station. When I told him I was just trying to help this handicapped lady, just showing respect for older people, he said he understood, but would still have to give me a ten-dollar ticket.

"Now ten bucks ain't much, but I'll tell you this: I was taught to respect older people, and I'd do it again tomorrow and the day after and the day after and the day after, even if it cost me ten bucks a whack.

"I don't think giving me a ticket was right, but when I have to do something to show respect for older people I'm going to do it. Look at it. They even sent me a letter saying I have to pay the ticket, and I'm going to pay to have five hundred of these run off and give them to all my friends, city councilmen, and everybody else. If I can't show respect for older people, then this is the wrong city for me. It's a principle with me. Ten dollars ain't much, but it's the principle. Older people are to be respected, and I was taught that all my life."

A five-minute lecture on respect, from a person I never expected to hear it from, but what an impact. He was not a rich man; he was not a handsome man; he was not a well-kept man. In fact, he didn't even smell good, but he was straight-on when it came to showing respect.

I couldn't help but think that God must have been pleased with cab driver number thirty-four. Here was a guy who knew about his responsibility to be respectful; and he was even willing to fight the police force and Mayor Mosconi in order to follow through with his conviction to show respect.

Respect is so important. If that word and the responsibilities it entails would stay near the top of your mind, your life would be much richer and your pathways smoother.

Remember our trip to Hawaii and how impressed we were with the manner in which the Hawaiians revered the elderly? The place of highest respect was reserved for the oldest male in the family, for he was considered full of experience and wisdom.

My first responsibility as a child was to respect and honor my mother and father. That is your responsibility as well. Sometimes, as parents, we don't merit your respect. We do foolish things, things that moms and dads should know better than to do. Sometimes we fail to respect you, and it's important that we learn to do that consistently.

Right now, we're trying to develop a healthy respect for your need of privacy. Respect for you should encompass an awareness on our part that you're a unique individual, a person whom we love, but an independent separate being, complete with your own free will.

God doesn't make a provision for not showing respect and honor to your mother and father. He attached a tremendous reward to respecting and honoring Mom and Dad. Consider the richness of this reward. God says, "Honor and respect your mother and father and you will be blessed by a long life" (*see* Exodus 20:12). Imagine that! If you honor your mom and dad and respect them, God promises to give you a longer time on this earth. The contrary is also true. God says, "Whosoever curses his mother and father his life will be put out in obscure darkness" (*see* Proverbs 20:20).

How do you show respect to Mom and Dad? You don't show respect by telling them, but through your actions:

- Respect is conveyed when you do a job without being asked.
- Respect and honor are shown when the job which is done is a quality one.
- Respect is shown when you follow their directions.
- Respect is shown when you spontaneously help, without even a request.
- Respect is shown by attempting to do those things which please.
- Respect is shown by doing things which take the burden from Mom and Dad.
- Respect is shown by representing the family well.
- Respect is shown by using good language, by being polite.
- Respect is shown by doing some things that they want you to do that you don't want to do, like taking piano lessons or cleaning your room or the garage.
- Respect is also shown through obedience.

Respect for those you'll encounter during the course of your life also has great significance. Respect for your employer is a necessity, for if you fail to respect him or do the things he has assigned, you will soon be jobless.

You've observed what happens at school when people lack respect. They steal the personal belongings of other people, they break windows, destroy equipment, and commit various other acts of vandalism. Some exhibit disrespect by using abusive language in public. This is offensive to many and often terminates friendships.

Our responsibility as parents is to set an example, so you may see us respecting our parents and all those around. I trust you've always observed us respecting our moms and dads. I also hope you've observed us respecting others and the rights they possess.

I know you've seen me fail, and you'll see me fail again and again; but, when I fail, I am responsible to only one Person: Jesus Christ. I, too, am held accountable for respecting other people; and I, too, will either reap the reward or suffer the consequences.

Nothing gives me a greater source of pride than to hear another adult say, "I am really impressed with your girls. They are so polite and show so much respect." My chest goes out until my buttons almost pop with pride.

Even if God had not promised a longer life to those showing respect and honor, you would easily see that respect and honor have other rewards. When I consider selecting a student for a special assignment, I only consider those who exhibit respect. When an employer considers a person for advancement to a higher position, he never considers a person who fails to show respect. When I select a teacher for employment at my school, I carefully inspect his references to see if they contain any incidents of recorded disrespect. Yes, Dawn, respect will open many doors and provide many opportunities. But the greatest fulfillment will come through knowing you've done what God directed you to do.

Love,
DADDY

Dear Daddy:

I've found that the amount of respect we show for others is the amount we are likely to receive in return. My problem is that I tend to judge others on their outward appearances and, based upon that, determine the amount of respect I show them. By your illustration, you taught me a lesson. Just because a person is unshaven, dumpy, or overweight, it doesn't mean they aren't worthy of our respect. They may add more to our lives than the person who meets all our standards.

I feel it is necessary to point out that God commanded us to respect our parents, not agree with them. I'm just beginning to realize this. Although at times I may not feel you are right, I still must honor your decision. This is difficult, but the rewards that follow make it bearable.

It is a lot easier for me to show respect for others when they exhibit respect towards me. I'm sure this is true for many people. Pray that I'll remember this the next time I begin to judge someone rather hastily or seem disrespectful or flippant when he or she is around.

Love,
DAWN

Sensitivity

Dear Dawn:

This afternoon your cousin Debbie came over to say, "Good-bye." She and her new husband, Casey, were departing for three years, to finish their college education in Kentucky. We knew we wouldn't be seeing them for a year or more.

As we discussed their future, in the family room, I glared at you, trying to catch your eye. You seemed very unsociable, said nothing, and never smiled.

When I sent you out for pizza, I followed you up the stairs and nailed you for your actions. Only when you broke down in my arms did I realize how deeply you were feeling the pending loss of Debbie. What I had construed to be a lack of interest and weakness on your part was actually a deep love for Debbie.

I didn't realize how deeply you were hurting, until later, when we walked Debbie to her car. Tears welled in my eyes and Mom's while we watched you and Deb, locked in each other's arms, sobbing. I thanked God at that moment for your tender heart and the deep feelings He gave you. I asked Him to increase my sensitivity and awareness to your strengths, rather than focusing on what I deemed to be your weaknesses. I wondered how many times before I had misjudged a strength as a weakness.

I'm thankful for your deep emotional feelings, for God gave them to you. They make you complete as a person. Never be ashamed of showing emotions, for they attest to your realness as a person.

When I see you cry at a friend's departure, laugh uproariously when I try to harmonize, get "goose bumps" during the national anthem, weep with joy when a person accepts Christ, freeze with concern as we pass an accident, run with open arms to meet Grandpa, tense up before a tennis match, tremble before that all-important oral presentation, or experience elation when we're about to depart on our vacation, I say, "Thank You, God, for giving her a full set of emotions."

I've observed some people who can sit through emotional experiences and remain totally unmoved. My heart goes out to them, for at the same time I've experienced a heartrending experience which has set me aglow from my head to my toes and will last at least a week.

Thank You, God, for giving my girls deep feelings. Let them feel proud and free to let these feelings demonstrate love, concern, and empathy for all who become a part of their lives. Help our home be conducive to letting us, and all who enter, freely express their feelings.

Thanks, Dawn, for crying, laughing, caring, and loving so visibly.

Love,
DADDY

Dear Daddy:
This holiday season brought so many strong feelings to the surface. It seems as though those past feelings become especially strong when my schedule becomes less demanding, allowing more time for reflection and thoughts of others. As you prayed at our family gathering on Christmas, many eyes

turned moist when you mentioned "loved ones who are away and unable to be with us." At that moment I thanked God for making Debbie such a special person whom I love so deeply.

I've learned that sensitivity involves many emotions, including some that are not so favorable. Losing Debbie to Kentucky, with the realization of how terribly I'd miss her, also made me aware of my selfishness in desiring that she'd remain. Sometimes sensitivity provides an excuse for hiding feelings of frustration, anxiety, envy, or jealousy. Although my emotions were sincere, negative sentiments crept in. I guess I really envied Debbie because of her recent marriage and the travel and adventure she'd encounter, but these feelings didn't lessen one bit the sincerity of the emotions I felt as she left.

Thank you for making me realize that sensitivity is not a handicap, but a strength. I sometimes say, "Why do I always cry at weddings?" or, "I wish I didn't cry when I feel patriotic," but then I think how stale the world would be without emotions. The different ways in which we react to situations keep each of us from becoming a carbon copy and add excitement and uniqueness to our lives and the lives of those around us.

I, too, thank God for a full set of emotions and His beautiful gift of sensitivity.

Love,
DAWN

Spirituality

Dear Dawn:

There are times when I feel as if I have no spiritual depth, and other times I feel very close to God. You've shared feelings with me that lead me to believe you experience these times also. It's not uncommon, on occasion, even to doubt whether there is a God. When you do this, you don't have to be guilt ridden. Simply ask God's forgiveness for doubting; He'll understand, and your relationship will actually improve as a result of your honesty.

I often make the mistake of judging a person's spirituality by outward appearances. In heaven I'll be surprised when someone whom I judged to be a flaky Christian is among those who receive the greatest rewards.

On occasion I've thought you were so wrapped up in the process of growing up that you didn't even think of spiritual things. Shortly thereafter, you asked a question which demonstrated you'd been dwelling on God's Word or principles for some time. How wrong I was, and how badly I had misjudged you.

Spiritualness is a personal matter between each person and his Saviour. You can usually observe things in a person's life which demonstrate his beliefs, yet you or I should not attempt to label him *spiritual* or *nonspiritual*.

Spiritualness in its highest form is a way of living and a

day-by-day experience. You talk to God all day long, throughout your activities, and consistently feel His presence and seek His guidance. The longer you nurture the spiritual, the more natural it becomes. Without a spiritual dimension, you lack completeness as a person.

I'm so pleased when I walk past your room and see you reading the Bible or praying. When you do this, you are developing a habit which will profoundly benefit you and those around you.

As life becomes more hectic and you assume more and more adult responsibilities, you'll have a tendency to think you're too busy for the Bible and prayer, yet that's precisely the time when it's the most important. The Word of God and the principles for living contained therein will have a decided impact on your life and will keep all of life in proper perspective. The Bible says, ". . . seek ye first the kingdom of God, and his righteousness; and all these things [everything else you need] shall be added unto you" (Matthew 6:33 KJV). God keeps His promises.

As you grow older, I trust you'll never grow too busy, too wise, or too independent to realize that God's Word contains within its pages all the answers to whatever problems you may encounter. As many years as I've been a Christian, I've never found God unable to remedy any problem I've brought to Him. When He hasn't solved it, it's only because I haven't given it to Him.

Part of physical growth entails becoming less and less dependent upon your mom and dad, yet part of growing spiritually is becoming more and more dependent upon your Lord and Saviour.

Keep on reading God's Word and praying.

I love you,
DADDY

Dear Daddy:

On many occasions I have felt envious of your relationship with God. That is why I sometimes act disgusted when you offer me verses of Scripture to help me cope with a problem. Please understand that I'm not angry at you, just disappointed in myself for not being as spiritual as I could be. I have to remember that, in order to get something out of a relationship, you have to put something into it.

It amuses, yet disappoints, me to see the "spirituality act" that so many of us exhibit today. We're all guilty of it, to one extent or another. Some of my friends are so holy at church, but when they get to school it's, "What's a Christian?" Little do they know, their actions can be deceiving and confusing to all those with whom they come into contact.

Thanks for understanding the doubt about God that sometimes overcomes me. When I say, "I don't even think You're there," it's so dumb, because I'm talking straight to Him when I say it. I believe that, with all the evidence of a loving God, it takes more faith to be an atheist than a Christian.

Thank you also for setting an example I can strive for.

Love,
DAWN

Truth and Honesty

Dear Dawn:

It's hard to think of anything more important than honesty and truth, for without them we have no standards by which to judge.

As a principal of a school, I daily observe students who lack respect for teachers whom they consider dishonest. The teachers who have student respect are the ones who feel free to acknowledge their shortcomings. They openly state, "I really don't know the answer to that question, but let's look together and see if we can find it." The teachers who receive little or no respect are those who'd never dare admit their knowledge was insufficient to field each and every question.

That's a good lesson to learn, for when we're dishonest in our responses to others, most of the people we think we're fooling can see right through us, and any respect they had for us is greatly lessened. Being dishonest also creates another problem, for one lie begets another, and soon the person telling lies is forced to continue in order to support the original lie. When you lie frequently, soon you don't really know what is truth and what is a lie, and therefore you're living in an unreal world.

One of the chief reasons for teenagers losing their jobs is lying or cheating. Cheating in school is common. In a recent poll, 67 percent of all ninth-grade students indicated they occasionally cheat in school. Most of them claim they cheat because they don't know the right answers, or the answers are really above their ability. Some say they cheat because they want a good grade. Others claim they cheat because they're afraid to flunk, for fear their parents will punish them. Some frankly admit, "I just didn't want to study." Whatever the reason, let me assure you that *nothing* justifies dishonesty and lying.

I often run into a problem with dishonesty in another way, and that dishonesty is called embellishment. Some people feel that others will not accept them unless they tell a story which is a little better than what actually occurred or exaggerate the circumstances. This is wrong and every bit as harmful as lying, and I have talked to you about my problem concerning this. Please make sure you guard against embellishment, for if a person doesn't accept you as you are, his or her friendship isn't really friendship.

Dishonesty also occurs through omission. When you know wrong has been done, or cheating has taken place, and, instead of admitting it, you refrain from offering the information, an act of dishonesty has been committed. I hope you have enough courage to come forth and tell the truth, even when it's difficult to admit that you've been dishonest.

The Bible says that, when we've wronged another person or told a lie, we should go to that person and tell him we've wronged him and seek his forgiveness.

As Christians we can also gain forgiveness through confession to God. First John 1:9 (KJV) says, "If we confess our sins [and certainly dishonesty is sin], he is faithful and just to forgive us our sins, and to cleanse us from all unrighteousness."

So, Dawn, that great Friend we have in Jesus is so interested in us that He'll forgive our dishonesty, renew our relationship, and give us a fresh new start.

A fine tribute is paid when one says, "If she said it, you can count on it." Making a commitment and failing to follow through with it is a definite demonstration of dishonesty. When you tell me you're going to do something, I know it'll be done, for your word is good.

Many parents, myself included, display dishonesty in other ways. On occasion I've told you to tell the telephone caller, "Dad's not at home." Other times, you see me drink wine with certain friends, yet refrain when Grandpa comes over. I know you're aware of these inconsistencies in my life, and I trust you'll forgive me for not being the model God wants me to be.

A subtle dishonesty which you may fall prey to is leading us to believe you're going to be home at 11:00 P.M. on the night you're staying with your girl friend, only to arrive at 1:00 A.M.

I feel confident that you are very honest and trustworthy. This pleases me greatly and makes me feel that others and I can rely upon you.

Thanks for being honest, open, and you.

Love,
DADDY

Dear Daddy:

I realize the important role honesty plays in any relationship; how can anything be sound if its foundation is falsehoods or half-truths?

I would be lying to you if I told you I've never cheated on a test in the past. My problem (well I guess it's really a blessing) is that I don't feel happy or satisfied when I get a good grade as a result of cheating. God has given me an ample ration of intelligence, and if I don't fully use it, it's wasted, and I am not everything I could be.

Some of the best advice Mom has ever given me was about how I should act on a job. She told me that if I honestly don't know the answer to a question or problem, I should openly admit it. This is very valuable advice. Bluffing my way through an answer doesn't do any good for anyone.

Thanks for giving me the guidelines for the positive and the cautions for the negative.

Love,
DAWN

Winning and Losing

Dear Dawn:

We all possess a keen desire to be winners. Many of our dreams revolve around our victorious emergence into the winner's circle. My dream was to be a basketball superstar, while yours might be to be crowned Homecoming Queen.

As much as we love to win, harsh reality dictates that for every winner there are multiple losers. Consider the fact that one team in the National Football League wins the Super Bowl, while twenty-seven lose. Those aren't the greatest odds.

In 1978 we watched the Dodgers spurt out to a two-game lead in the World Series, only to suffer the Yankees winning the next four games, totally humiliating the Dodgers. You were devastated at the losses, and for a short period you appeared very depressed. I'm glad you feel deeply and have such a keen sense of loyalty, yet I hope you don't attach too much importance to winning and losing.

Having been a coach for five years, I considered the ideal competitor one who demonstrated his love for winning by expending his best effort, yet one who could also lose graciously and profit from his loss. There is a lesson to be learned from every losing situation, if we evaluate our performance and alter our future behavior, based upon what we learn, yet too frequently the loss sends us into so deep a tailspin that we wallow in self-pity, which prevents us from ever sorting out the lesson to be learned.

One prayer I have for you girls is that you'll win often. Mom and I trust you'll achieve the honors you're working for in school, get the job you apply for, obtain the position of leadership you're competing for, marry the man you're attracted to, and achieve the life goals you arrive at. But an even more important prayer is that you may be able to accept the losses which you'll experience in life as "temporary changes in direction," with no devastating effects.

We often interpret situations wherein we fail to get what we applied for as losses. Christians, however, should view these "losing" situations as road signs designed to change their paths in a slightly different direction which will ultimately lead to increased happiness and fulfillment. The Bible says, ". . . all things work together for good to them that love God, to them who are called according to his purpose" (Romans 8:28 KJV). This means even the losses have a purpose in their lives and will eventually work for their good. I know it's hard to believe that at times, especially immediately following the loss; but, if Scripture says it, we know it is true.

The Holy Spirit within us acts as a guidance system directing our paths, if we are sensitive to Him. Often what we consider losses are really roadblocks designed by our God, to make certain we're directed into more profitable pursuits.

Realizing Jesus Christ has conquered death, the ultimate loss, and lives within us to care for every detail of our life and has promised us eternal life with Him, can we really consider ourselves losers? We are all winners, regardless of our present circumstances. Please remember this.

Go Dodgers! (Next year's another year.)

Love,
DADDY

Dear Daddy:

At least you can't say I don't have any competitive spirit. In fact, my supply is overabundant! I realize, myself, that I do get too involved.

I hope your input about losing will prove very helpful in the future. I shouldn't view my losses as failures. As a Christian, God assures me that both winning and losing play important parts in developing me into a complete person. If I catch my faults and resolve to change them, my failures might actually prove to be more worthwhile than my successes.

Please pray that God will help me control my sometimes unhealthy competitiveness. But, if the Dodgers don't win this season. . . .

Love,
DAWN

Whistle While You Work

Dear Dawn:

There comes a time in everyone's life when he has a strong desire to find a job and earn his own money. Employment offers you the promise of increased independence and the ability to purchase all those things you always wanted but Mom and Dad said you really didn't need.

That first job also helps settle those doubts about whether you can convince an employer that you are good for his business, whether you can perform well and master all those new instructions he's given you, and, in general, whether you're good enough to make the grade. It's normal that you have these doubts, for almost every teenager does. I know that you're plenty good, but now you'll have the satisfaction of proving it to yourself.

That first paycheck is a real thrill but also has a potential to create many problems. The most serious problem one acquires when paychecks start rolling in is that of believing the purchase of things will produce happiness. Let me tell you: Things do not bring happiness. Many adults, including your dad, have fallen into the trap of accumulating more and more things, then finding out that things produce but momentary happiness. When you finally have all those things stockpiled, you're trapped and continually have to work in order to support and maintain all those things you've accumulated. Acquiring things may seem great at the moment, but having your life programmed by those things is a real bummer. Some people get so involved in things that they can't even take advantage of new opportunities, for fear any change in their lives will result in losing some of those things they've worked so hard to obtain.

I hope you guard against getting trapped by things. I'm not saying it's wrong to have nice things, but make certain, Dawn, that you keep them in proper perspective. Don't let acquiring things become one of your chief goals, for, if and when it does, you'll never achieve the same satisfaction from your association with people.

Another problem with accumulating things is the maintenance they require. Nothing is more tragic than to see a person spending all his leisure time taking care of things rather than participating in activities which would allow him to grow.

Things can even stand between you and Jesus. For He has said, "Love not the world nor the things that are in the world, for if any man loves the world, the love of the Father is not in him" (*see* 1 John 2:15). He also says, ". . . seek ye first the kingdom of God . . . and all these things shall be added unto you" (Matthew 6:33 KJV). In other words, Jesus is saying if you keep Him in the proper perspective and the place that He should have in your life, He'll give you everything you need.

I've never been able to understand why God allows some people to have an abundance of things, while others barely have the necessities of life. However, I've seen people who have more than I could imagine, who were totally miserable; and I've seen people with hardly anything, who seem to have a handle on all of life and fulfillment.

As soon as some people are employed, they worry about advancement. "Now that I work in a bookstore, when will I become manager?" There's one rule you should always remember. If you do your best job in your current position, advancement will take care of itself.

Some young people will never advance in their area of employment, since they don't have the correct attitude. They believe older people to be outdated and inferior in intelligence. As a result, they don't respect them.

When you don't respect adults, you have serious problems. God has told us that we should respect people in authority over us. This applies to the president, government officials, teachers, parents, and employers. If you do not respect your employer, you'll never make it in the working world.

Numerous items are important when you begin work, and I hope we have instilled these attitudes in you through our home life. Be neat; be respectful; be punctual; always do your best job; be courteous; when the heat is on, be calm; be kind; begin each day with love; always expect the best of another person; be honest, your honesty will be appreciated.

One of the highest rewards that we will ever be given will occur when we stand before Jesus Christ and hear Him say, "Well done, thou good and faithful servant." You know, Dawn, He may even look at our employment record when He makes that statement, and I know that you'll have positive marks in that column.

Love,
DAD

Dear Daddy:

My desire to work in order to acquire spending money surfaced earlier than I expected it would. After a few, "I'm sorry but we aren't hiring now's," I began to sense a feeling of hopelessness and lack of worth. I wondered how everyone else managed to get a job. What a joy I felt yesterday as I called you from a large shopping center with the news that I had been hired as a salesperson. Thinking back, I can now understand why God waited for a few months, because of other conflicts, before allowing me to work. At the time, however, it was difficult for me to understand His reasoning.

There is one aspect involving my work that I must share with you. Last summer I felt very pressured by you and Mom to get a job. At the time, I wasn't ready for that kind of responsibility. That feeling of pressure made me shy away from working. Perhaps, without it, I would have gotten a job sooner.

Thanks for the warnings about the power of money. I'll be sure to exercise caution in these areas.

Right now I'm nervous about the training which begins tomorrow. Pray that I'll remember, "I can do all things through Christ who strengthens me!" (*See* Philippians 4:13.) Pray, too, that I'll keep Christ first as I become active in the working world and take advantage of any opportunities He presents.

Love,
DAWN

P.S. The orientation went great! It's going to take a while before I feel completely comfortable in this position, but I'm going to give it my all. Working today filled me with the feelings of self-worth and independence. It also totally wore me out, so, if you'll excuse me, I'm going to bed.

P.P.S. Two weeks later—Working adds a new dimension to life. It introduced me to many interesting people and activities. Despite the first week, when I came home every night saying, "I'm going to quit, or I should be fired by tomorrow," I'm glad for the experience of being part of the working world.

Today a Skateboard, Tomorrow 390 Cubic Inches

Dear Dawn:

A short time ago you learned how to drive. What a thrill for you! When I was confident you could handle the responsibility, I was proud to hand over the keys. That vehicle can contribute much to your life in terms of enjoyment and independence. Without your dad or mom as supervisor while driving, you're in control of your own destiny.

Although driving offers so many positive possibilities, it could also be the most destructive privilege you've ever earned. Every time you get behind the wheel, you are in control of a two-ton weapon whose potential for destruction is awesome. A running child can be wiped out instantaneously; oncoming passengers in approaching cars can lie lifeless in a moment; and, most important to us, your life hangs in the balance.

You can't afford to be frivolous or careless. You must guard against the desire to perform for your friends, who may be encouraging you to do so. You must guard against emotional overreactions while driving. Drivers will cut you off and wrong you in other ways which will make you angry, but you must now realize that reaction in anger will have consequences far greater than "being grounded," or losing other privileges.

I had to carefully observe your ability to handle anger-producing situations in a mature way before I forked over the keys. You see, driving is a privilege, not a right. It must be earned. Once earned, you must continually demonstrate your ability to deserve the privilege, or it will be revoked.

The sensitivity you have is beautiful. Your emotions and deep feelings for people please me and add great dimension to your life. This same sensitivity would haunt you if you wiped out a life with your car.

So, my dear, remember above all that every passenger you carry in your car, every pedestrian you pass, every occupant of every approaching car, is deeply loved by someone. And as my heart would be broken if you were injured, maimed, or killed, someone else's would be, also.

Love,
DAD

Dear Daddy:

You have stressed the responsibility of driving, from the first frustrating day we hopped and lurched around the high-school parking lot. After many weeks of practice, the final obstacle—the driving test—approached. Somehow I had the feeling that you were as nervous for me as I was for myself. What a relief it was to share the joy of passing the test with you. It was even more exciting for me when you handed over the keys, and along with them, the responsibility you had talked about. The day I had waited for for sixteen years had arrived. The first time you permitted me to use the car alone, I felt a greater degree of trust than I had ever experienced.

Then, a month later, came that terrible day when I rolled back into someone at an intersection. No damage was done, but the experience seemed tragic to me. I thought my life was finished. As I drove home, I trembled at the thought of the conversation that would have to take place.

When I told you what had happened, your response was entirely different from what I expected. You were concerned about me, not the car. After assuring me everything was fine, you asked me to run some errands for you. I'm just now beginning to realize how important it was for me to get right back into that car. Not once was your voice raised or punishment inflicted. God used that accident and the way you responded to it in a way that again reinforced your statement about responsibility. Thanks for continuing to trust me and the new set of car keys.

Love,
DAWN

P.S. Each time I'm about to drive, I know what's coming: "Be careful, Dawn." While I know you mean well, it's kind of irritating to hear your reminder over and over again, especially in front of my friends. At times I'm still embarrassed about it long after I've left the house. Now that I've told you how seriously I take my driving responsibility, maybe you won't have to tell me, "Be careful," so often. You know I will be, anyway.

Another Man Will Take My Place

Dear Dawn:

It's difficult for me to write this note, since at present I'm the most important man in your life. Your love for me is special; I can feel it. I hope you feel my love as strongly as I feel yours.

From the day I peered at you through the nursery window in the maternity ward, until today, as I view you standing on the threshold of adulthood, you've been Daddy's baby. And you should know I'll feel that way about you my entire life. Whether you're within arm's reach or halfway around the world, whether you're ninety pounds or obese, a housewife or a surgeon, you'll always be my baby. There's something special between us, and we'll always have it to share.

But, Dawn, there will come a day when I will stand at the front of the church and will be asked the question, "Who giveth this woman away?" and I'll answer, "I do." Vows will follow, during which time you'll pledge your love to another man, and he to you.

This is God's plan for most people, and Dad will rejoice with you. God has said it is natural for a man and a woman to leave their mothers and fathers and cleave to each other. But I will also be very concerned, because for the first time you'll be out from under my roof and my responsibility. Questions will fill my mind. Will he take care of her as I did? Will he love and cherish her? Will he respect her? Will he work hard to provide for her? Will he encourage her? Will he protect her? Will he be a good father? Will he be faithful to her?

My dear, if the answers to these questions prove to be *yes,* I'll handle being the second-most-important man in your life very well. I'll even look forward to becoming number three or four in your life, if you're blessed with a son or two.

Even now I frequently pray that God will bless the man He's picked out for you and prepare him to have all the attributes that will provide you with happiness and fulfillment. I also pray God will use your current experiences to prepare you to be a young woman capable of enriching your marriage, while making your husband feel loved and important as he guides your relationship and family. No one on earth could be more important to your husband's success than you. If, through your attitude, actions, and loving spirit, he knows you're pleased with him and supportive, your combined chances for fulfillment and a successful marriage will be greatly enhanced.

Be assured that when you're married, number one will be accepted and loved and prayed for by number two, because he's taking care of Daddy's girl and becoming an integral part of her life and mine.

> *Love,*
> YOUR CURRENT NUMBER ONE MAN

Dear Daddy:

There are times when I don't believe this statement is valid. But, someday, I hope to find a new number one. (I can't deny it!) You've got to understand I've been your number two, or number three, or number four, for my whole life. It is important to feel needed and wanted in a special way only a husband can provide.

Some of my fondest memories of you are when we sat down and talked after I've gone out with a boy. I remember laughing with you as I described one date's car, clothes, and mannerisms. It is so neat to be able to share this important part of my life with you.

If I remain single, you'll always be my number one. But, if I do find someone I want to share the rest of my life with, I know you'll gladly take the backseat. You see, I want to be someone else's number one also.

Love,
DAWN

Marriage

Dear Dawn:

You may eventually marry; or you may choose to remain single. Most of the topics we've discussed are applicable, regardless of your choice.

I trust you'll be patient and take ample time before jumping into marriage at too early an age. Assuming marriage may be for you, I encourage you to pray every day that God may be preparing you for marriage, as well as the man who will eventually be your husband. It's not too early to be making this important decision a matter of prayer.

A lengthy courting period usually provides an opportunity for both people to view each other in joyous as well as trying circumstances. Seeing one respond to a variety of situations provides a sound basis for interaction and determining whether you'd like to be married to that person for the rest of your life. We used to laugh as we discussed Aunt Grace and Uncle Charlie's eight-year engagement, yet a long engagement may be far better than too short an engagement, when it comes to deciding upon your life partner.

Dr. Jim Dobson, noted psychologist, indicates that if he had his way, he'd prefer people marrying only after they've reached their twentieth birthday. I concur. While some teenage marriages are successful, the rate of divorce among those marrying in their teens far exceeds the mortality rate of later marriages.

God's Word and your father encourage you to marry a young man who loves God as you do. God's love shared by two people is something special. It provides a basis on which a sound marriage can be built and also allows you to be more sensitive to each other's needs. Once you marry, you have the capability of making your marriage a success or dooming it to failure.

Whether you work for an employer or inside the home, the pressures on a young couple to keep their marriage in harmony require a total commitment. No marriage will survive, much less grow to fulfillment, without a concerted effort on your part and that of your mate.

Before you marry, spend long hours talking about what you both expect from marriage, and more important, what you're willing to do in order to achieve those expectations.

When two people believe they're in love, there's a tendency to gloss over or avoid probing potential problems, for fear it will demonstrate a lack of love or trust. Without discussion, you proceed into marriage assuming your deep love will smooth out all the rough spots. As the surprises unfold and result in relationship problems in those early years, you'll realize you should have discussed your feelings and beliefs much more thoroughly before marrying.

Enough adjustments come upon you naturally in marriage, without further compounding the situation by failing to discuss questions similar to the following:

- Does it matter where we live?
- How do you feel about not living near your parents?
- Do we want children?
- If we do, when?
- Do we both want to continue working?
- What do you feel strongly about?

- Are you content to live without the niceties until I finish school?
- Will we accept help from our parents?
- What are your feelings on finances?
- How important is honesty in our relationship?
- Is attending church important to you?
- How do you feel about my chosen work?

Many other questions can be added to this list, but a thorough discussion of these and other vital subjects is necessary to assure as smooth as possible an adjustment to marriage. Premarital or engagement-encounter counseling may also prove helpful in identifying areas for discussion.

After determining that your potential mate shares your spiritual faith, shares similar expectations for your marriage, shares many of your views on the subjects discussed, has reacted to the good and bad times in your courtship in a manner with which you feel comfortable, you must then decide whether or not you love him and he loves you enough to spend the remainder of your lives together.

While, at this juncture in your life, love may lack the maturity which develops with time spent together, you can test yourself by asking the following questions: Do I care for him almost as much as I do for myself? Does he feel the same about me?

If all else checks out and you can answer the two preceding questions *yes,* you probably have a sound basis on which to enter the marriage relationship.

A sound marriage is a gift of God and one of His rich blessings.

Love,
DADDY

Dear Daddy:

Recently, several family friends have had their marriages end in divorce. I know now that engagement and marriage are not to be taken lightly.

Today so many marriages flounder. I believe this is so because people are entering into marriage with the idea that they can easily be released through a divorce. While divorce was once considered inexcusable, it is now widely accepted.

I, too, agree that age is important to a successful marriage. Yes, teen marriages can succeed, but, if two people are meant for each other, a few months or years shouldn't alter their love. Marrying another Christian is essential. If my whole life centers around Christ, how can a marriage be complete without a husband who shares the same goals and beliefs?

You and Mom provide an excellent example of a healthy marriage. Mind you, I didn't say *perfect,* just *healthy.* One of the neatest things you've ever told me was when you recently shared that your marriage had "never been better." The reassurance and faith in marriage which those words brought me was incredible. Marriage *does* work, if those involved are willing to.

Thanks for the guidelines.

Love,
DAWN

Death and Taxes

Dear Dawn:

While we're on earth, most of us make a conscious effort to avoid thinking of or mentioning death. We are so busy contently living and enjoying life that we hesitate to turn our minds toward this event which faces us all as part of life. Why talk about something that's unpleasant, that causes grief, until you absolutely have to face its reality?

It is estimated that most families can go through a period of twenty years without confronting death in their family. Others aren't so fortunate, and they must face death.

Our hearts went out to the family in our church that recently lost a three-year-old boy. Remember the solemnness that came over our entire family as we realized this young, vivacious boy, who probably had sixty or sixty-five more years to live, was struck down and would never reach his potential?

I believe it's unhealthy to not know where you stand concerning death, until you're faced by that situation. How much healthier it is to have examined the subject while you're able to unemotionally view its reality.

As a child of His, there is no way that I can discuss the subject of death without also discussing the reality of heaven. At one time, talking about life after death would have been considered foolish by our present-day society. However, recent books, such as *Life After Life,* by Raymond A. Moody, Jr., and works by Elizabeth Kubler-Ross, have indicated that doctors and scientists are now discovering the fact that, indeed, there must be life after death.

As Christians, we sometimes get the feeling that because we know the deceased person was a Christian and will be spending eternity in heaven, we shouldn't really feel bad about his death. This is not the case. Any natural response to death is healthy: grief, tears, a tremendous feeling of loss, all are normal and healthy. The only limitation from God is that when we grieve, "We should not grieve as those who have no hope" (*see* 1 Thessalonians 4:13). Just recently we lost Grandpa, after his bout with cancer. Remember the tears and grief that all of us suffered? These feelings and emotions are normal and natural and nothing to be ashamed of. After losing Grandma, I had a strong desire to be alone for long periods of time, just to reflect upon the good times and experiences she had brought into my life.

Even as children of God and people who love Him, it is not unnatural to question His wisdom at this time. We may even question His love. "God, why did You take this person from me? He meant so much to me. Most people live seventy years, and he didn't live nearly this long." Such questions are common, and I believe God does not begrudge answers to our honest questions. We should state these concerns to God. God respects honesty and provides a special measure of grace to handle the hurt in our times of need.

It is natural to go through a period of guilt after the death of a loved one. As we reflect upon the times we've had with that person, things will come into our mind which we could have done more effectively for him. Most people also experience a tendency to evaluate their future performance upon what the deceased person would have wanted. "I wonder what Dad would have wanted in this case," is asked by many a child who has just lost Dad. There is also a normal tendency to make the person appear better than he or she actually was. While these tendencies are normal, they become abnormal when we dwell on them to such a degree that they affect our future productivity. As His children we have the opportunity to commit these concerns to God in prayer, and He will assist in the healing process. He will take away the fears. He will fill the void. He may even bring other people into our lives, for the purpose of comforting and healing.

One meaningful way to assist ourselves in handling the death of a loved one is to seek other people who need help and invest our energies to supplying this help. Helping others significantly aids our own healing process.

Honesty is important in dealing with death. Remember when we walked into the funeral parlor and saw Grandpa's body in the casket? Seeing his body that way, for two days before the burial, is truly viewing death honestly.

Some people approach death dishonestly by saying, "He's not gone; he's really sleeping," or, "Although he's not here, his presence is here." We must face the fact that death is truly a separation. You will not see that person again on earth. Praise God, we, as Christians, have the assurance that we will spend eternity with our loved ones.

As you visit people who have just lost their loved ones, it is difficult to find words. A sincere expression of sorrow, a hug, a kiss, or any other nonverbal expression of love, says, "We care," and is often far superior to any stumbling verbal attempt to console the person who suffered the loss.

In his book entitled *The View From a Hearse*, Joseph Bailey states, "Time heals grief; love prevents scar tissue from forming." And nothing is more important during the time following death than the love and acceptance of other people.

You have often asked me, when we lost an animal, whether

or not that animal would go to heaven. You then asked what the difference was between an animal and a person. If an animal doesn't go to heaven, how could we be sure a person does?

In *The View From a Hearse,* Joseph Bailey explains the situation this way.

> For an animal, death is like going to sleep when you're really tired. Know how good that feels sometimes? As far as we know an animal never wakes up. We bury the animal in the ground to show our love for it, and because if we didn't, it would spoil and get flies on it and maybe spread disease.
>
> But a person is different. A person goes to sleep, too, when he dies, but he wakes up afterward. And if he loves God, he wakes up in a wonderful place called heaven. This is God's special home, though God is everywhere.
>
> When a person dies, his spirit leaves his body, in which it has always lived. A spirit is the real person, the part of us nobody can see, the part that doesn't die. It's the inside you that says, "God, I love you," when you don't even move your lips; that makes you glad when you obey and unhappy when you don't; maybe it's the part of you that remembers, that dreams happy dreams, that feels warm and cozy when you're sitting on Mother's lap.

The death of a loved one who is a child of God can often be viewed this way. For some reason, Jesus Christ wanted the departed loved one to be in His presence at that time. As simplistic as this might sound, what a tremendous reality to realize that that person we loved so dearly is also loved so dearly by Jesus Christ that He wanted him in His presence.

Dawn, I have the perfect assurance that Jesus Christ has conquered death. You remember, in the Bible, that Jesus wept when Lazarus died; then He proceeded to raise Lazarus from the dead. Other incidents in the Bible were recorded in which Christ actually granted people additional years on earth to complete a purpose which He had for them. There is no question that He has the power to heal and extend life.

Yes, although I know you'll question His wisdom as He takes a loved one from you, I trust that, after thinking about it, you'll be able to say, "Jesus, I trust Your wisdom in taking that person from me, and although I hurt deeply and feel the loss, I commit that person to Your presence."

Our family has been fortunate enough to have not suffered any loss as far as children are concerned. Joe Bailey lost three children, but yet could come to the realization:

> We don't own our children; we hold them in trust for God, who gave them to us. The eighteen or twenty years of provision and oversight in training that we normally have represent our fulfillment of that trust. But God may relieve us of this trust at any time, and take our child home to His home.

You've asked me on occasion, "Why would a God who is supposed to be love cause pain and suffering in death?" I've never really been able to answer that question, but I have some thoughts which I'd like to leave with you.

We can't always understand the infinite actions of a loving God. But our peace and comfort are not based on being able to understand the situations we may find ourselves in: Our peace should be found in the realization that God is in control of everything that occurs in our life.

God is a sovereign God. He does not make mistakes. Sometimes we question His decisions, and this is normal. At times we rationalize and say God must have allowed this death because of this reason or that, but that is all a guess on our part. We must come to the place where we realize that He does not base His decisions on our ability to understand. God has told us that these situations would come into our lives. He has never promised that being a Christian would mean that we could bypass the trying experiences on earth. He intends that we will be stronger and our character built up through some of these suffering situations, for how we respond in these critical situations can be a powerful testimony to the reality of our faith.

You've asked me what happens when the body dies. I believe that when the body dies, our spirit, the nonmaterial part of us that really is our inner person, will immediately go to heaven to be with God.

Even when the doctor is performing an autopsy, or when the funeral director is embalming our bodies for display in the caskets, our spirits are already with Jesus Christ. While our loved ones are grieving in the funeral chapel, we are one with God Himself in heaven.

After our bodies are buried, the deterioration process starts; and, as the Bible says, we were created from dust and our bodies will deteriorate to the state of dust.

The second stage is going to occur at some future date, when Jesus Christ returns to claim the people who have accepted Him as their personal Saviour; when this happens our bodies will reunite with our spirits. They will be changed bodies, bodies similar to that of Jesus Christ. They will be bodies that will not die, will not feel pain, will be healthy, and through which we will be able to glorify Christ.

I quote from Joseph Bailey again:

After His resurrection Jesus Christ had a body that was somehow different from the one that had been lovingly taken from the cross and placed in the tomb by His friends. It was His body, recognizable, including nail prints in the hand; yet it possessed a glory beyond.

This reunion of the individual spirit with the body He shed at death reconstituted and glorified, will take place at the time of Jesus Christ's second coming to the world.

You've asked me whether or not we really know there's a heaven. My answer to you in all honesty is, "No." I don't really *know* there is a heaven, because I have not experienced it, but the latest scientific evidence even reveals that there is a heaven. When a number of people who were clinically announced dead and then recovered were interviewed, many of the people indicated that they had seen loved ones and God Himself, in glimpses of heaven. This is reported by a highly credible doctor: Elizabeth Kubler-Ross.

But even if this scientific evidence were not coming into the forefront today, I accept the reality of heaven by faith in Jesus Christ and upon His authority, for He has stated, "In my Father's house are many mansions: if it were not so, I would have told you. I go to prepare a place for you. And if I go . . . I will come again, and receive you unto myself; that where I am, there ye may be also" (John 14:2,3 KJV).

Dawn, please realize that death is only a temporary state, that Jesus Christ has conquered death because of His death on the cross of Calvary, and that when we, as a family, lose loved ones, or when we ourselves depart, we can be assured that we will be reunited with one another when Jesus Christ returns.

You have often asked, "Will we recognize each other in heaven?" The answer is an unqualified, "Yes." Our personal identities will be known to one another. The Bible recounts the fact that Elijah and Moses, who had been dead for centuries, both appeared with Christ on the Mount of Transfiguration, and their identities were known by the disciples.

During life, you'll be questioned, from time to time, about your beliefs concerning death and heaven. Some skeptics may even laugh or scoff at your beliefs, but be strong and remember Jesus Christ was raised from the dead, and that is true. If it were not true, He would not have had the impact upon our world that He has had for centuries. If God can raise Jesus Christ from the dead, certainly He has the power to raise us from the dead and reunite our bodies with our spirits and take us to heaven to spend eternity with Him.

I have carefully examined many explanations, and I have comfort in the fact that what Jesus Christ said is true. I'm glad you have accepted it as truth and that we will have an opportunity to spend eternity together, for I love you dearly.

> *Love,*
> DAD

Daddy:

Death is a subject that frightens me. I know this feeling is irrational but, nonetheless, it's impossible to erase. I am a Christian and believe in heaven, but the unknown and unexperienced still scare me. When I was younger, I used to hope someone would send me a letter from heaven, assuring me all was as it was said to be.

Recently, after three years of suffering, a friend of mine lost her mother. The death left my young friend with five children to raise. Although I loved her dearly, I seemed to feel resentment as she asked me to attend the funeral. Now I realize that the emotion causing me to feel that way was fear, not resentment. I consented because I thought I owed it to her. What a mistake! The way her family accepted their mother's "graduation" and praised God for it blessed me far more than the extent to which I could have comforted them. Thank you, friend, for allowing me to celebrate with you.

At the death of Grandpa, I found myself feeling tremendously guilty because of the relief I felt. The doctors had diagnosed terminal cancer, and with his death came relief both for himself and his family. Maybe the release brought through Grandpa's death was a form of comfort from the Holy Spirit, for it allowed us to rejoice in the fact that he now had a new body, free from sickness.

I am just beginning to realize death can be a celebration experience. Sure, we'll miss that person and all he's meant to us, but he's experiencing the highlight of his life, basking in the light of the One who created both life and death. I know it's useless to tell you not to grieve when I die, but please realize it's what I'd want you to do. Focus on the time when we will meet again, in His glory.

I love you so much.

DAWN

If You Falter

Dear Dawn:

I've given you much advice over the years, but I know it's much easier to give advice than to follow it. I have faltered and failed to follow my own advice, and that of my father and mother, on many occasions. It's just so easy to know what to do, but so hard to actually do it. In the Bible, Paul stated it well when he indicated that those things he knew he should do he often didn't do, but often found himself involved doing those things he knew he shouldn't do. (*see* Romans 7:19).

When you feel as if you've really blown it, your heavenly Father waits for you, with outstretched arms, to receive you, forgive you, comfort you, heal you, and bathe you in His love. You've got to be careful, however, not to misuse the knowledge that He stands ready to forgive you. It's easy to say, "Since I know He'll forgive me and welcome me back, I'll choose to do those things I know are wrong." This would be the wrong use of God's grace, and I know that you do not wish to abuse it.

Teenagers often struggle with decisions, not knowing which way to turn. Please don't ever hesitate to come to me and talk to me because of embarrassment or because you think you're about to fail. Let's discuss it. I'll try to accept you where you are and, hopefully, I'll be able to bear some of your burdens, while supporting you in prayer. Never forget that you, too, have the resource of prayer. As a child of His, God stands ready to guide you, give you wisdom, and provide strength for you to handle different decisions you will need to make. All you have to do is call upon Him.

Even though you have this resource, you'll occasionally falter and make the wrong decisions and be deeply grieved, as a result. This is normal and doesn't mean your worth as an individual is lessened. I want you to know that I stand waiting, like God, to welcome you back.

God forbid that heartaches will be prevalent in your life, but even those heartaches that you now feel, I feel. I want you to know you'll always be welcome in my arms, regardless of the circumstances. Even when I've warned you about the consequences and you've gone ahead in spite of my cautions, resulting in great concern and hurt in your life, I want you to come back into my arms. You are my flesh, and nothing can take you out of the realm of my love. From the moment I first viewed you until the day I depart from this earth, you are in my love. Whether you're fifty years old, are married and have children of your own, or come to me next year, you'll always be a vital part of my life and love.

My love is not contingent upon your making the right decisions. Certainly I'll be disappointed if over and over again you make decisions that harm you, but my love will be there continuously.

Teenagers fail to use their parents as a resource, but turn instead to their friends for advice and consolation. I'm glad you have so many good friends and can turn to them in the time of need, yet please realize that my bonds and love for you go deeper, and I will always endeavor to help you, regardless of the situation, because you are part of me, and we are part of God.

Remember, no matter what situation you find yourself in, two things are constant: God's love and your mom and dad's love. Turn to us when you need us. We'll be there.

Love,
DAD

Dear Daddy:

Finally a chapter I feel very knowledgeable about, for I often falter. Fortunately, though, through my experience I have discovered one important rule: You can't change the past, so instead concentrate the effort wasted on worrying or regretting on the future. Perhaps the added energy applied will then correct the problem or will increase your chances for success. Even if it doesn't, your effort is not wasted.

Thanks for bringing out the fact that we can misuse God's forgiveness. I've met people who want to show how merciful God is by disobeying Him, thus demonstrating His grace. I know this is the wrong approach. As Christians, we should strive to be more like Christ, not do our own thing and expect Him to "clean up our act."

Thank you also for assuring me of your constant love. I know kids that would pay for the parents God gave me—free!

I love you,
DAWN

Differences

Dear Dawn:

A human relationship without differences has never existed, for each of us is unique. Even as I read what I've written to you and your responses to me, it becomes evident that our relationship, as mutually satisfying as it is, reflects some divergence of feelings, philosophies, and opinions.

Certainly some differences are attributable to our age difference, some a result of your being a girl and me a middle-aged man, and some the result of us both being created by God as unique individuals, complete with our own perceptions, feelings, free will, creativity, and personality. How blessed!

Differences can either be the catalysts which eventually destroy a relationship, or they can provide a strengthening bond. Love is the ingredient which determines whether differences have a negative or a positive effect upon a relationship. Because we love each other so much and communicate freely with our feelings, we are aware of our differences and strive to view each situation from each other's perspectives. As we become keenly aware of each other's feelings and needs, we also grow more sensitive to others around us. As this happens, your life will bridge to others, and they in turn will sense your awareness and seek you out for companionship.

Some people believe that those involved in a close relationship should surrender their uniqueness and strive for sameness. I disagree heartily. Many friendships and marriages become distastefully boring when both members become so eager to please that they fail to take a definite stand on *any* issue. This practice is every bit as dangerous as one mate dominating the other while attempting to mold his spouse into his predetermined ideal. Danger also exists whenever a person possesses strong feelings, yet is unable to freely express them, for fear of rejection. The deeply harbored feelings, when allowed to accumulate, often build to the point of an irrational explosion, threatening the entire relationship.

The differences you've expressed provide a source of comfort to me, for they assure me of your emerging strength and growth towards independence and your increased ability to examine all aspects of a situation before forming an opinion. The ease with which I can finally take "hands off" will be proportionate to my belief in your decision-making ability. Independent decision making is absolutely necessary to survival in life.

Some teenagers pride themselves on always adopting a position opposite their parents'. Whether the intent is to prove their independence or to express rebellion has never been quite clear to me. While I'm thankful for, and respect, our differences, I also rejoice in the fact that we share similar views in many vital areas.

My greatest cause for rejoicing comes from the commonality we share in Jesus Christ. The Word of God is often subject to individual interpretation, but it does not allow for differences when it comes to the subject of eternal life.

Many believers, however, are driven apart while focusing on their differences rather than dwelling on their commonality (the shed blood of Christ), which evidences itself in a bond of love. I love you and trust you have tasted of my love through the many years we've spent together and the many experiences we've shared. I respect your right to differ with me, for I possess no superhuman qualities that insure me against mistakes. Each day reinforces my humanness, as I see where I have erred. The only one who merits Lordship and a reputation for perfection is the God you and I worship.

You have been, and continue to be, a vital part of my life. I'm sure our love will grow even stronger as we're privileged to spend more years together. We've shared some precious times together. You may remember some of them. I've held you all night when you've been sick! I've worried for you when you had fears; I've laughed with you when you've been tickled; I've played with you; I've wept with you when you were heartbroken; I've swelled with pride at your accomplishments; and I'm sure many emotional and meaningful situations are yet to come. Situations like these have cemented our relationship.

I believe our relationship is sound because we've practiced the three Rs:

Recognize—We recognize the fact that differences are a normal and expected part of every relationship.

Reconcile—We work to reconcile those emotionally charged differences which possess the potential to wreck our relationship. Compromise from both parties is usually necessary in this process.

Respect—We've learned to value and respect those differences which may bother us but seem to be an indelible part of the other party's life. Tolerance, bathed in love, often changes potential problems to appreciation.

Thanks, God, for our differences and thanks for the privilege of being a dad.

Love,
DAD

Dear Daddy:

I read this chapter over a couple of times and didn't know how to respond to it. Frustrated, I put it aside. Shortly thereafter, I made a phone call to a friend, in an attempt to resolve some problems we had been experiencing. In the course of our conversation, she said, "Dawn, we both have our differences, but with God's help they can strengthen our relationship." Right then, I realized what my hang-up was. I had always thought of differences in negative terms, not positive. I had been trying to conform my friend into a mold, never thinking that perhaps her uniqueness had something to offer me.

Thanks, Daddy, for illustrating that differences are blessings and thank you, Rynea, for helping me write this letter!

Love,
DAWN

What the Future Holds

Dear Dawn:

At times, I lie awake at night and wonder what your future holds.

- Will you attend college or begin your life's work upon completion of high school?
- Will you marry or remain single?
- If you marry, who will your husband be: a teacher, a doctor, an accountant, a pastor?
- Will your husband love God, as you do?
- Will you have a happy and fulfilling marriage?
- Will you have any children? One, two, or more?
- Will you face serious illness?
- Will you remain close to God or become too busy for Him?
- Will you be possessed by a love for material things or content with whatever you have?

Question after question roams my mind, yet I know only time will reveal the answers.

As your dad, I trust I've played an important part in your life and will continue to do so.

I love God's Word. It's so important to me. Even as I face the reality of your maturing and leaving my home, I find comfort in the Bible's assurance that I can still have a positive impact on your life, through my prayers.

Whether you're here in California, or halfway around the

world, take comfort in knowing that a day will never pass without your dad praying to his heavenly Father on behalf of his daughters.

Dear Lord

Thanks for giving me the privilege of fathering three daughters.

Thank You for the love we've shared and the enrichment and fulfillment they've brought to my life through joys and sorrows.

Bless their relationships with others, but most of all with You. Give them a hunger for You and Your Word, that they may daily experience the reality of knowing what You meant when You said, ". . . trust the Lord completely; don't ever trust yourself. In everything you do, put God first, and he will direct and crown your efforts with success" (Proverbs 3:5, 6).

I love you and always will,
DADDY

Dear Daddy:

At times, I lie awake at night and wonder the same things! Thanks for the assurance that you're always there and praying for me, no matter what happens. Thanks, too, for the forgiveness you have freely offered me when I've made mistakes and disappointed you. You have played an extremely important role in my life; and, despite my actions at times, I appreciate the corrections and guidance you have offered. Thanks, most of all for being my dad.

I love you and always will,
DAWN